STECK-VAUGHN SOCIAL S

People and Places Nearby

Teacher's Guide
Level B

ISBN 0-8172-6557-0

Steck-Vaughn
C O M P A N Y
ELEMENTARY • SECONDARY • ADULT • LIBRARY

ACKNOWLEDGMENTS

Executive Editor: Diane Sharpe

Project Editor: Janet Jerzycki

Assistant Art Director: Cynthia Ellis

Design Manager: John J. Harrison

Program Development, Design, Illustration,
   and Production: Proof Positive/Farrowlyne Associates, Inc.

Contents

The Philosophy of Steck-Vaughn Social Studies

Social studies focuses on developing knowledge and skill in history, geography, anthropology, economics, and political science. Most importantly, it focuses on people and their interaction with each other and the world in which they live. *Steck-Vaughn Social Studies* addresses these areas of study in a six-level program that correlates with the social studies curriculum throughout the United States. This program can serve as an alternative to traditional basal textbooks. *Steck-Vaughn Social Studies* helps students acquire the skills, knowledge, and understanding they must have in order to function as concerned and involved members of our society.

Steck-Vaughn Social Studies is a program that both you and your students will enjoy using. Its approach is based on widening the horizons of students as they progress through the elementary grades. Students will gain a concrete, understandable framework for learning the principles of democracy and citizenship. They will also gain a better vantage point from which to view the world's diversity.

ABOUT THE PUPIL EDITIONS

The individual features of *Steck-Vaughn Social Studies* have been designed to help students meet with success in their study of social studies. A variety of features work together to create books that are both inviting and manageable for students who have difficulty reading in this content area.

Format

The pupil texts are divided into units and chapters of manageable length. Each unit opener identifies the important concepts of the unit and sets the stage for successful reading by asking questions to spark student interest. A photograph welcomes students to each new unit. The unit opener also suggests an idea for an appealing cooperative learning project for students to carry out as they read the unit. The unit closes with suggestions of ways students can complete and present their project.

Interactive Activities

Activities on the pupil edition pages ensure student involvement by asking them to respond to the text. Many of the activities emphasize geography skills. Activities also include recall questions, higher-level thinking questions, and activities that require student interaction with maps, charts, and illustrations.

Readability

A readable and manageable text draws students into the content and ensures their understanding. The text never talks down to students or overwhelms them, but rather respects them and presents the content in a form they will understand and enjoy. Difficult concepts are presented in a straightforward manner. The students' prior knowledge is used as a starting point for presenting new concepts. The reading level is carefully controlled at or below grade level in order to ease the difficulties students often have with reading content-area materials.

Text	Reading Level
Level A	Grade 1
Level B	Grade 2
Level C	Grade 2
Level D	Grade 3
Level E	Grade 3
Level F	Grade 4

Vocabulary

Key social studies terms are boldfaced and defined in context in the texts. The glossary at the end of each book lists the terms and their definitions alphabetically.

Special Feature Pages

These pages appear at the end of every chapter and focus on a person, place, or event that extends the chapter content. For example, "Around the Globe" special features in Level C take students to Australia and Canada. In the chapter about ancient Egypt in Level F, the "Special People" feature focuses on Hatshepsut. One "For Your Information" in Level E extends the content of the Civil War with a description of the Freedmen's Bureau set up to help African Americans after the war.

History Strand

Steck-Vaughn Social Studies addresses the often neglected need for history in the lower grades. For example, students at Level A read about the first families in the United States—American Indians and Pilgrims. At Level C, students explore the development of a community—Omaha, Nebraska—from the days of the Omaha people to the present.

Skills Program

Each unit includes social studies and geography skills such as maps, globes, charts, and graphs as part of its narrative content. A Skill Builder at the end of each unit extends the content, at the same time reviewing a social studies or geography skill taught previously in the unit.

Maps and Illustrations

Students are drawn into the texts by abundant maps and illustrations that enhance their understanding of the content.

Chapter Checkups

Checkup tests provide successful closure to each chapter. The consistent format helps students feel comfortable in a review situation. Each Checkup consists of questions in standardized test format, which address the factual content of the chapter. A critical-thinking-and-writing question that requires students to display their deeper understanding of a chapter concept concludes the chapter.

ABOUT THE TEACHER'S GUIDE

The separate Teacher's Guide presents strategies for units and chapters with guidelines and answers for the interactive text; mid-term and final tests; letters to families; and useful graphic organizers.

Teaching Strategies

The unit strategies include a unit summary, pre- and post-reading activities, guidelines for implementing the unit project, and bibliographies for both teacher and student. In addition, references to the Teacher's Resource Binder blacklines are included, should you choose to purchase this additional resource.

The chapter strategies include activities for pre- and post-reading, as well as a chapter summary, objectives, a list of vocabulary along with vocabulary activities, and page-by-page teaching suggestions and answers to interactive text.

These activities can help teachers accommodate the individual and group needs of students.

Letters to Families

Family letters are provided for every unit of Levels A, B, C, and D, and for each book of Levels E and F. The letters invite families to participate in their child's study of the book and provide suggestions for some specific activities that can extend the concepts. A separate Spanish version of each letter is also provided.

Assessment and Evaluation

A mid-term and final test are provided in the Teacher's Guides for Levels C, D, E, and F. The tests are in the standardized test format familiar to students from the Chapter Checkups.

To implement portfolio assessment, invite students to select samples of their best work to supply for their portfolios. Ask them to tell you which work they are most proud of and why. You may want to suggest that students' work on the cooperative learning unit projects be considered for their portfolios. Allow students to discuss with you any work they would like to change and how they would change it.

CONTENT SCOPE AND SEQUENCE

	LEVEL A	LEVEL B	LEVEL C
HISTORY	• People, families, and neighborhoods change over time. • American Indians were the first Americans. American Indians helped the Pilgrims to survive. • National holidays and patriotic symbols remind us of our heritage.	• American Indians were the first Americans. • Christopher Columbus came to America in search of new trade routes. • American Indians helped the Pilgrims survive in America. • Neighborhoods change over time. • Holidays commemorate special events and people from our history.	• American Indians made up our nation's earliest communities. • Pioneers settled on American Indian land and built communities such as Omaha, Nebraska. • Thanksgiving celebrates an event in American history. • Each community has its own history that we can research.
GEOGRAPHY	• Families live in homes of different sizes and shapes. • Different families need or want to live in different places (near rivers, mountains, etc.). • A globe is a model of Earth. • Earth provides us with many resources.	• Neighborhoods are real places we can show on maps. • Globes are ways of showing the whole, round Earth. • Neighborhoods around the world are both alike and different. • There are seven continents on Earth. • Earth has different geographic features such as mountains, plains, rivers, and oceans.	• Life in communities often depends on natural resources, climate, and landforms. • Water is a very valuable natural resource. • Plains and mountains are important landforms. • The American Indian way of life was shaped by the land.
GOVERNMENT / CITIZENSHIP	• Rules help us to live, work, and play at home and in the community. • We have responsibilities in our families. • Families share feelings about their country and about their flag. • It is important to take care of the environment. • Families remember great Americans and events on special days.	• We live in the United States of America. • Neighbors work together to solve mutual problems. • Rules and laws tell us what to do and what not to do. Rules and laws help us live together. • Groups have leaders (mayor, governor, President).	• A community is run by a government. • Government leaders are elected by the people of a community. • Communities have laws to tell people what to do and how to act, to protect people, and to provide safety. • Our national government is based in Washington, D.C.
ECONOMICS	• People work to earn money to buy the things they need and want. • Some people produce goods and others provide services. • We can't always have everything we want. People make choices as to which needs and wants they will satisfy.	• Some people produce goods and others provide services. • Workers cooperate to produce goods. • People use the money they earn to buy the things they need and want. • The choice of jobs may be limited by the place in which a person lives. • Taxes help pay for many community services.	• As workers, people are producers; as buyers, they are consumers. • One product may be produced by many people working in different communities. • Communities depend on one another. • Jobs and industry determine whether or not a community will grow or shrink.
SOCIOLOGY / ANTHROPOLOGY	• Families vary in size and structure. • Families provide for physical and emotional needs and wants. Different families have somewhat different rules and private holidays. • Schools are special places for learning. • All family members can help the family meet its needs and wants.	• Neighborhoods are places in which to live, work, and play. • Neighbors vary in age, language, and other human characteristics. • People share the customs of their homelands with new friends and neighbors in the United States. • Neighbors share local and national holidays.	• Communities vary in size: rural towns, suburbs, and cities. • People live, work, and play in communities. • Living in communities makes it easier to get things done and to help people. • We have American traditions. • We also have many individual family traditions.

CONTENT SCOPE AND SEQUENCE

	LEVEL D	LEVEL E	LEVEL F
HISTORY	• The American Indians were the first to settle in what is now the U.S. • The U.S. has always been a nation of immigrants. • The geography and natural features of a region affect the course of its history.	• The history of the U.S. tells how different groups built a strong nation. • U.S. history can be divided into several distinct periods. • The study of these periods shows how people and events have shaped the present. • The study of the past shows the development of important ideas.	• Civilizations in Asia, Africa, Europe, and the Americas made key contributions to human life and knowledge. • The ancient Greeks and Romans and the nations of Western Europe have influenced many nations. • Geography, trade, and technology can affect the development of a civilization.
GEOGRAPHY	• The U.S. is a large nation. It includes 50 states and Puerto Rico. • The Northeast, Southeast, North Central, Rocky Mountain, Southwest, and Pacific regions are groups of states with characteristic geographic features. • Landforms and climate influence the way people live and work.	• The U.S. has diverse landforms, climates, and natural resources. • The U.S. can be divided into several distinct regions. • The geography of the U.S. has affected the ways in which the nation was explored and settled. • U.S. geography has influenced economic activities.	• Varied land regions, climates, resources, and bodies of water are found on Earth. • People adapt differently to different natural environments. • Latitude, altitude, and ocean currents can affect climate. Climate affects cultures. • A wise use of resources is necessary for a healthy environment.
GOVERNMENT/ CITIZENSHIP	• The U.S. is a democracy in which voters are free to choose their leaders in local, state, and national governments. • Each level of government handles different kinds of problems and functions. • Americans share pride in a heritage they have built together.	• The U.S. is a democracy. • The U.S. Constitution contains the beliefs of the colonists about freedom, equality, justice, and property. • It establishes the branches of the government. • The Constitution (including the Bill of Rights) has been the basis for the rights of Americans.	• Governments vary from dictatorships to democracies. • Ancient Greek and Roman governments influenced our own. • The roles of citizens can vary from no participation to making many political choices. • Economic upheavals and new political ideas can change government.
ECONOMICS	• Americans do many jobs that are created by the U.S.'s wealth, natural and human resources, education, and freedom to make choices as interdependent consumers and producers. • Transportation and communications systems allow the exchange of goods and materials produced in different places.	• Americans have several ways of acquiring goods, services, and property. • Natural resources and technology have influenced economic activities in different U.S. regions. • Changes in transportation and communication have affected economic activities.	• Nations trade with one another to obtain needed raw materials and goods. • Economic development is affected by a nation's government, resources, technology, trade policies, and trade practices.
SOCIOLOGY/ ANTHROPOLOGY	• Individual Americans, though diverse in occupation, family heritage, and other human characteristics, share certain American customs, languages, and symbols.	• American Indians had developed cultures before the arrival of European settlers. • Different groups have made contributions to U.S. society. • American traditions influence our approach to issues such as minority rights and conservation of resources.	• The values and beliefs of a culture influence its growth and development. • The culture of a society includes its customs and religious beliefs. • Advanced cultures have writing, art and architecture, science, and mathematics. • Trade and war can lead to the diffusion of cultures and to new cultures.

SKILLS SCOPE AND SEQUENCE

	LEVELS:	A	B	C	D	E	F
GEOGRAPHY AND OTHER SOCIAL STUDIES SKILLS	Understanding globes	8	4	8	14		2, 12, 18
	Understanding time zones						1, 17
	Using map keys	7	1, 4, 9	1, 2, 12	1, 4, 6, 8, 10, 12, 13	3, 4, 5, 6, 8, 10, 11, 13, 14, 16, 17	2, 4, 7, 8, 10, 14, 19, 20
	Using scale and distance			1, 2, 12	4, 5, 10, 11, 14	2, 5	6, 9, 15, 16
	Working with directions	6, 7, 8, 9, 10	1, 4, 9, 11	1, 2, 3, 4, 5, 6	1, 4, 6, 7, 8, 10, 12, 13, 15	2, 8, 9	9
	Working with landforms	8	1, 5	2, 5	1, 4, 5, 7, 8, 9, 10, 11, 12	2, 17	2, 12, 16, 17, 18
	Working with latitude and longitude						2, 12, 16
	Working with maps	7, 8, 9	1, 4, 9, 10, 11	1, 2, 3, 4, 5, 6, 10, 11, 12, 13, 14	1, 2, 4, 5, 6, 7, 8, 9, 10, 11, 12, 13, 14	1, 2, 3, 4, 5, 6, 8, 9, 10, 11, 13, 14, 16, 17	1, 2, 3, 4, 5, 6, 7, 8, 9, 10, 11, 12, 13, 14, 15, 16, 17, 18, 19, 20
	Working with graphs	6	5, 7	9, 11	2, 3, 11	11, 12, 14	15, 16
	Working with time lines		12	13	13, 15	2, 5, 6	9
	Working with charts	11	3, 9	9, 11	7	2, 4, 7	6, 10
	Working with diagrams			8, 12, 15	3, 14		
	Working with tables				6		
THEMATIC STRANDS IN SOCIAL STUDIES	Culture	1, 2, 3, 4, 5, 6, 7, 8, 9, 10, 11, 12	1, 3, 4, 5, 6, 7, 8, 9, 10, 11, 12	1, 2, 3, 4, 5, 6, 7, 8, 9, 10, 11, 12, 13, 14, 15, 16	1, 2, 3, 5, 6, 7, 9, 10, 11, 12, 13, 14, 15	1, 2, 3, 4, 5, 6, 7, 8, 9, 10, 11, 12, 13, 14, 15, 16, 17, 18	1, 2, 4, 5, 6, 7, 8, 9, 10, 11, 13, 14, 15, 16, 17, 19, 20
	Time, continuity, and change	1, 4, 6, 7, 9, 10, 11, 12	2, 3, 4, 10	1, 3, 6, 9, 12, 13, 14, 15, 16	2, 3, 5, 7, 8, 9, 10, 11, 13, 14, 15	1, 2, 3, 4, 5, 6, 7, 8, 9, 10, 11, 12, 13, 14, 15, 16, 17, 18	1, 4, 5, 6, 7, 8, 9, 10, 11, 13, 14, 15, 16, 17, 18, 19, 20
	People, places, and environments	1, 2, 3, 4, 5, 6, 7, 8, 9, 10, 11, 12	1, 2, 3, 4, 5, 6, 7, 8, 9, 10, 11	1, 2, 3, 4, 5, 6, 7, 8, 9, 10, 11, 12, 13, 14, 15, 16	1, 2, 3, 5, 6, 7, 8, 9, 10, 11, 12, 13, 14, 15	1, 2, 3, 4, 5, 6, 7, 8, 9, 10, 11, 12, 13, 14, 15, 16, 17, 18	1, 2, 3, 4, 5, 6, 7, 8, 9, 10, 11, 12, 13, 14, 15, 16, 17, 18, 19, 20
	Individual development and identity	1, 2, 3, 6, 7, 8, 9, 10, 11, 12	4, 6, 7, 8, 9, 10, 11, 12	1, 3, 4, 5, 6, 8, 9, 10, 11, 12, 13, 14, 15, 16	2, 3, 4, 7, 9, 11, 13, 14, 15	1, 3, 4, 5, 6, 7, 8, 9, 10, 11, 12, 13, 14, 15, 16, 17, 18	4, 5, 6, 7, 8, 9, 10, 11, 13, 14, 15, 16, 19, 20
	Individuals, groups, and institutions	1, 2, 3, 4, 5, 6, 7, 8, 9, 10, 11, 12	1, 2, 3, 4, 5, 6, 7, 8, 9, 10, 11, 12	1, 3, 4, 6, 7, 9, 10, 11, 12, 13, 14, 15, 16	3, 4, 5, 6, 9, 10, 11, 12, 13, 14, 15	1, 2, 3, 4, 5, 6, 7, 8, 9, 10, 11, 12, 13, 14, 15, 16, 17, 18	1, 4, 5, 6, 7, 8, 9, 10, 11, 13, 14, 15, 16, 17, 19, 20
	Power, authority, and governance	1, 2, 3, 4, 5, 6, 7, 8, 9, 12	6, 7, 8, 9, 10, 11	1, 2, 3, 7, 9, 10, 11, 12, 14, 15, 16	3, 7, 9, 11, 13, 15	3, 4, 5, 6, 7, 8, 9, 10, 11, 12, 13, 14, 15, 16, 17, 18	1, 4, 5, 6, 7, 8, 9, 10, 11, 13, 14, 15, 16, 17, 19, 20
	Production, distribution, and consumption	3, 4, 5, 8, 10, 11	3, 4, 5, 6, 7, 9	1, 3, 5, 7, 8, 12, 13, 14	5, 6, 7, 8, 9, 11, 12, 13, 15	1, 3, 4, 5, 9, 10, 11, 12, 13, 14, 15, 16, 17, 18	1, 3, 4, 5, 6, 7, 8, 10, 11, 12, 13, 14, 15, 16, 17, 19
	Science, technology, and society	1, 4, 5, 7, 9	2, 5, 7, 10	1, 4, 7, 8, 10, 13, 14	1, 7, 9, 13, 14, 15	2, 3, 10, 11, 12, 13, 14, 15, 16, 17, 18	1, 3, 4, 5, 6, 8, 9, 10, 11, 13, 14, 15, 16, 18, 20
	Global connections	2, 3, 6, 8, 9, 12	1, 3, 4, 5, 10, 11, 12	5, 6, 8, 11, 16	2, 4, 5, 6, 7, 8, 10, 12, 14, 15	1, 2, 3, 5, 6, 10, 12, 15, 16, 17, 18	1, 2, 3, 4, 6, 7, 8, 9, 10, 11, 13, 14, 16, 17, 19
	Civic ideals and practice	4, 5, 6, 7, 9, 12	4, 5, 7, 8, 9, 10, 11, 12	1, 3, 7, 8, 9, 10, 11, 12, 13, 14, 15, 16	3, 4, 7, 9, 13	3, 4, 5, 6, 7, 10, 11, 12, 15, 17, 18	3, 4, 5, 6, 8, 9, 10, 11, 15, 16

Unit Summary Neighborhoods exist all over the world. Although neighborhoods may differ, they all share certain features. Neighborhoods change because of technology, because people move, or because buildings are torn down, repaired, painted, and replaced.

Before Reading the Unit Invite students to look out the window and describe what they see. Ask questions to help students think about the buildings and people they see. Next have students look at the unit opener page. Ask them to describe the people in the photograph and what they are doing. Tell students that people who live in a neighborhood often play together. Ask students what game the children in the photograph are playing. Then ask students to read the page. Have a volunteer read the questions aloud. Tell students that they will find the answers as they read the unit. Point out the Unit Project box and tell students that they will work on a project as they study the unit.

Unit Project

Setting Up the Project You may wish to have students focus their work on the neighborhood surrounding your school. Guide them on a walking tour of the neighborhood to help them get started. Have students bring along pencils and paper. Pause occasionally to allow students to take picture notes and draw maps.

Students will find specific suggestions for their project in the Project Tip in each chapter. Encourage them to adapt the suggestions to their own interests.

Presenting the Project Students can follow the suggestions on page 21 or choose other ways to present what they have learned. One alternative is to have students create a mural that shows specific places where people live, work, and play.

After Reading the Unit Ask students to look back at the questions in the unit opener. Invite students to give answers. Prompt additional discussion by asking questions such as: What are some of the ways that our neighborhood is like other neighborhoods? Where do people live and work? What is the land like in our neighborhood? Are there bodies of water such as oceans, rivers, or lakes near our neighborhood?

Skill Builder

Using a Map

Before students read the Skill Builder on page 20, discuss the benefits of knowing how to read a map. Help students understand that mastering this skill can help them learn about their neighborhood and help them show friends where places are.

Answers: 1. Students should put an *A* over the airport. **2.** Students should circle the house that is west of the post office. **3.** Students should draw a picture for a school in the map key and on the map. **4.** Students should draw a line south from the airport to the post office.

Bibliography

Teacher

Ellis, A. K. *Teaching and Learning Elementary Social Studies.* 4th edition, Allyn G. Bacon, 1991.

Heck, Denis Lyn Daly (ed.). *Barrios and Borderlands: Cultures of Latinos and Latinas in the United States.* Routledge Press, 1994.

Natoli, S. (ed.). *Strengthening Geography in the Social Studies.* National Council for the Social Studies, 1992.

Student

Humphrey, Paul. *Foods from Friends and Neighbors.* (Read All About It Series) Steck-Vaughn, 1995. (Grade 2)

Keller, Jack. *Tom Edison's Bright Ideas.* (Real Reading Series) Steck-Vaughn, 1992. (Grades 1–2)

Lye, Keith. *Mountains.* (What About? Series) Steck-Vaughn, 1995. (Grades 2–3)

Palmer, Joy. *Deserts.* (What About? Series) Steck-Vaughn, 1995. (Grades 2–3)

Palmer, Joy. *Oceans.* (What About? Series) Steck-Vaughn, 1995. (Grades 2–3)

Taylor, Barbara. *Mountains and Volcanoes.* (Kingfisher Young Discoverers Series) Kingfisher, 1993. (Grades 3–4)

Teacher's Resource Binder

Blackline Masters for Unit 1: Unit 1 Project Organizer, Unit 1 Review, Unit 1 Test; Activities for Chapters 1, 2

Chapter Summary People who live near each other are neighbors. A neighborhood is a place where people live, work, and play. Neighborhoods can be in or near many different kinds of places, such as mountains, plains, rivers, and oceans.

Chapter Objectives Students will learn to

- identify and define *neighbor* and *neighborhood*.

- read a picture map with labeled symbols.

- use a map key.

- identify and use cardinal directions and a compass rose.

- identify major landforms: mountains, plains, rivers, and oceans.

Vocabulary

neighbors, p. 6	directions, p. 9
neighborhood, p. 6	mountains, p. 10
map, p. 8	oceans, p. 10
map key, p. 8	plains, p. 11
compass rose, p. 9	rivers, p. 11

Vocabulary Activities Ask students to brainstorm all the words they can think of that relate to the word *map*. You may want to use the Concept Web graphic organizer found on page 48 of this guide for this purpose. Suggestions for getting students started include: roads, streets, houses, highways, directions. If students have difficulty with any of the vocabulary words, help them use the glossary to review the terms.

Before Reading the Chapter Point out to students the various maps contained in the chapter. Review the different views presented on a picture map and on a map with symbols. Have students tell how the two kinds of maps are different. Ask students if they know what type of land they live on (mountains, plains, hills, prairie, and so on). If you live near a body of water, ask students to give its name and to identify it as a river, a lake, or an ocean.

Teaching Suggestions and Answers

Page 6

Guide a discussion about the neighborhood where your students live. Prompt students by asking: Who are your neighbors? What kind of work do they do? What kinds of homes do they have? Help students understand that many different kinds of people live in a neighborhood. Ask students to name places in their neighborhood where people work. Have them tell about places where people play. What else do people in their neighborhood do?

Page 7

Lead students on an imaginary walk through the neighborhood pictured on pages 6 and 7. Encourage them to identify the different activities they see neighbors doing together. Help students see that neighbors are working and playing together. **Students should circle places in the picture that they have in their neighborhood. Student responses to what the neighbors are doing together may include: skating, raising the flag, building a snowman, sled riding, playing ball, using playground equipment, attending a wedding.**

Page 8

Ask students how a map of a neighborhood can be helpful. Elicit that a map can help people find their way around, remember where places are, and tell others how to find places. It can also show what places are nearby or far away. Ask students how knowing whether a place is near or far can help them. In discussing the map key, stress that the pictures, or symbols, stand for any house, any post office, or any library. **Students should put a checkmark next to the picture of the house on the map key. They should identify the picture of the book as the symbol for a library.**

Page 9

Students should circle all the pictures of houses. Explain that a map shows what places are near each other and which places are far away. Discuss with students why knowing what is near and far is useful. **Students should place a checkmark next to one of the places near the Art Museum: the music school, church, or neighbors.**

Draw a picture of the compass rose on the chalkboard and then have students find the one on the map. Guide students in finding the sides of the map that correspond to the four cardinal directions. **Students should draw a line under the park, which is north of the library.**

Page 10

Point out the oceans on a world map or a globe. Invite students to tell what they know about oceans. Compare the oceans to lakes on the map to help students appreciate how large the oceans are. Invite students to tell what they know about mountains. Explain that mountains are found in several parts of the United States. Point out mountainous areas on a map of the United States. **Students should place an X above the picture on the right of the mountain neighborhood. They should respond that warm clothes are needed in the mountains because it is cold.**

Page 11

On a United States map, point out areas where there are plains, explaining that much of the land in the middle part of the country is made up of plains.

Discuss the differences between rivers and oceans. Explain that rivers are found in mountains and on plains. Guide students in identifying several rivers on a United States map. Point out any that are near where students live. **Students should circle one of the photographs.**

Project Tip

Help students describe where their neighborhood is located. You might sketch a map of your neighborhood on the chalkboard and assist students in locating mountains, oceans, or rivers that might be nearby.

Page 12

Around the Globe Have students compare the two photographs. Ask them how they know the photographs are of neighborhoods in different parts of the world. Help them recognize the tropical settings, the differences in how people dress, the different types of homes and buildings. **Students should respond that the two neighborhoods are alike because people live and work in both neighborhoods.**

Page 13

Chapter Checkup You may want to work through the Chapter Checkup with students. Make sure they all understand what the correct answers are to the numbered questions.

Answers: 1. plains **2.** mountains **3.** compass rose **4.** map key
Answers will vary. Accept all reasonable answers.

After Reading the Chapter

Provide students with old magazines and ask them to find and cut out pictures of neighborhoods in or near mountains, on plains, near rivers, and near oceans. Have them work together to make posters for each of the landforms by pasting the pictures on poster board.

Art

Invite students to draw a picture of their favorite place in their neighborhood. Display the drawings on the bulletin board and encourage students to tell about the places and why they like them.

Geography

Students might make a map or picture of the neighborhood around their school.

Writing

Have students think about how their neighborhood changes from season to season. Ask them to write two or three sentences about each season, telling how the neighborhood is affected.

Chapter Summary Neighborhoods change over time. A neighborhood of 100 years ago looks very different from a neighborhood of today. Some of the differences are caused by advances in technology. More specific and short-term changes also occur in neighborhoods, such as those caused by people moving into and out of neighborhoods and fixing or replacing buildings.

Chapter Objectives Students will learn to

- identify a neighborhood of long ago.

- compare a neighborhood of long ago with a neighborhood of today.

- identify ways in which neighborhoods change over time.

Vocabulary

inventions, p. 15

Vocabulary Activities Ask students to name inventions they know about. Make a list on the chalkboard. After students have compiled a list, emphasize to them that almost everything they see around them was invented by someone. Be sure students understand the difference between inventing something and making something that has already been invented. Then challenge students to draw a picture of something they would invent. Encourage them to use their imaginations. When finished, have them show and explain their pictures to the class.

Before Reading the Chapter Have students bring in photographs of themselves as babies. Students should point out three ways they have changed and one way they have stayed the same. If there is some construction under way in your neighborhood, discuss the events with students. If possible, bring in photographs of the work in progress. Remind students, or show them with photographs, how the area looked before construction began. Work with them to list some of the changes that are occurring.

Teaching Suggestions and Answers

Page 14

You may wish to discuss with students their understanding of "long ago." Emphasize that 100 years ago is long before students' grandparents were born. You might point out that 100 years ago automobiles had only recently been invented and airplanes had not yet been invented. Have students study and talk about the picture. **They should draw a line under the pictures of horses and horses pulling carriages, people wearing old-style clothing, the blacksmith shop and dry goods store.** Ask students what things in the picture could be found in a neighborhood today. Students should recognize that houses, fences, and trees look much the same today.

Page 15

Encourage a discussion of changes in the neighborhood by asking questions. Which two houses from long ago are still standing? (The white house in the center on the front street and the yellow house on the back street just left of center) What has happened all around them? (Apartment buildings and businesses have been built, first small ones and then larger ones) Why have the changes come about? (More and more people moved in and there were advances in technology.) Invite students to tell whether they think the changes to the neighborhood are good or bad. Together with students, make a list on the chalkboard of methods of transportation used long ago. Make another list of methods of transportation used today. Discuss with students the differences and similarities of the types of transportation people have used over the years. As students read and look at the pictures, have them identify forms of transportation. Have volunteers write and illustrate each type of transportation on the chart. Have students add other forms of transportation that they know about. **Students' answers may include the way in which automobiles have changed how people move from place to place, and how new methods of construction have changed the places in which people live and work. Students** should circle any one of the changes shown in the picture on this page.

Page 16

Students should put an *X* on the broken and missing windows and shutters, the trash, and the broken mailbox. They should circle one thing they would fix first. Answers will vary. Ask students how fixing the house will change the neighborhood. They might answer that it will make the neighborhood cleaner, better looking, and a nicer place to live. Challenge students to look very closely at the picture and tell how they think the rest of the neighborhood might look. You might suggest that other houses are also for sale and need repairs. Point out the "for-sale" sign in front of the neighboring house and the boarded-up window.

Page 17

Tell students to look at the picture on page 16 at all the things they found that needed fixing. Have them compare those things to the picture of the same house on this page. Have all the things been fixed? **Students should write a *C* on all the things that have been changed.** Ask students to look again at the picture. Besides fixing the house, what other changes have been made around the house? Students should notice that flowers have been planted. Invite students to discuss how planting flowers, trees, and shrubs can make a neighborhood look nicer.

Project Tip

Help students brainstorm a list of changes that happen in a neighborhood, such as widening streets, building new parking lots, planting trees, constructing new sidewalks, damage from fires and storms, dying trees, and so on. Make a list on the chalkboard of types of changes. Then have students work in small groups to compile a list of specific changes they have observed in their neighborhood.

Page 18

Special People Invite students to share what they know about Thomas Edison. Tell them that he made more than 1,000 inventions during his life. Among them were the movie projector, the phonograph, and alkaline storage batteries. Help students understand how Edison's inventions have changed the way people live.

Mention that Edison was a very practical man. He always tried to make sure that his inventions would not break easily and could be used by ordinary people. Edison was also very modest; he was the first person to admit that being an inventor was hard work. After experimenting with thousands of different ways to get a storage battery to work, he announced that he had not failed but had succeeded in finding 10,000 ways that wouldn't work! **Answers will vary. Possible answers might include that they could not read, play some games or sports, practice hobbies, eat at restaurants, visit with friends, or go shopping after dark.**

Page 19

Chapter Checkup Make sure all students understand what the correct answers are to the numbered questions.

Answers: 1. T **2.** F **3.** T **4.** T **5.** F
Ask students to share their ideas. Possible answers might include that more people move in or out; new buildings are constructed or old buildings are removed; businesses open or close; buildings are painted; trees are planted.

After Reading the Chapter

Plan a trip to a senior citizen center to interview a few of the older members of your community. Help students think of questions to ask about their community's history and how the community has changed.

Geography

Ask students to work in small groups and draw a map of their neighborhood as it looks today. Then have the students do research and ask questions to learn how the neighborhood has changed in the past 25 or 50 years. Using this information, have students draw another map of their neighborhood as it looked in the past.

Writing

Have students write about one change they would like to see made in their neighborhood. Ask them to tell how they think the change would make their neighborhood better.

Unit Summary American Indians were the first people to live in America. How they lived varied from group to group. In 1492, Columbus came to America. His journey to America and the subsequent arrival of English settlers changed this land in many ways.

Before Reading the Unit Have students look at the picture on page 22. Ask students what words and phrases describe the picture. Explain to students that the view shown in the photograph probably looked much the same hundreds of years ago. Ask students how people have changed the way the landscape looks. What kinds of things do people build that change the way the landscape looks today? (highways, tall buildings, cars, ships, telephone and power lines) Then ask students to read the text and to think about the questions. Tell them to look for answers to these questions as they read the unit. Have students read the Unit Project box.

Unit Project

Setting Up the Project You may want to do some advance research to learn which American Indian groups lived in your area and to determine whether suitable materials are available for student research. You might contact a local historical society or library to see if you can arrange to borrow materials.

Remind students that they will find specific suggestions in the Project Tip sections of the chapters. Students should adapt the suggestions to their own interests.

Presenting the Project One alternative to the suggestions on page 37 would be to have students share with another class what they have learned about the American Indian groups. Your class could divide responsibilities for telling about life within the group.

After Reading the Unit Ask students to review and discuss the unit opener questions. Prompt additional discussion by asking questions such as: Were all American Indians the same? Did they eat the same foods? Did they live in the same kinds of houses? Why do you think the American Indians helped the Pilgrims? How did the Pilgrims thank the American Indians for their help?

Skill Builder

Reading a World Map

Before students read page 36, review what they have learned about using a compass rose to find directions. Ask a volunteer to remind the class of the difference between continents and oceans and to tell how many continents are shown on a world map.

Answers: 1. Atlantic Ocean **2.** Students should put an *X* on Mexico. **3.** Students should put a *C* on Europe. **4.** west

Bibliography

Teacher

Cohen, Elizabeth G. *Designing Groupwork.* 2nd edition, Teacher's College Press, 1994.

Low, Alice (compiler). *The Family Read-Aloud Holiday Treasury.* Little Brown, 1991.

National Geographic Society. *Story of America.* National Geographic Society, 1992.

Slater, Frances. *Learning Through Geography.* NCGE, 1993.

Student

Bennett, Paul. *What Was It Like Before Electricity?* (Read All About It Series) Steck-Vaughn, 1995. (Grade 2)

Hankin, Rosie. *What Was It Like Before Television?* (Read All About It Series) Steck-Vaughn, 1995. (Grade 2)

Humphrey, Paul, and Alex Ramsay. *What Was It Like Before Cars?* (Read All About It Series) Steck-Vaughn, 1995. (Grade 2)

Jacobs, Daniel. *What Does It Do? Inventions Then and Now.* (Ready • Set • Read Series) Steck-Vaughn, 1990. (Grade 2)

Spencer, Eve. *Three Ships for Columbus.* (Stories of America Series) Steck-Vaughn, 1993. (Grade 2)

Stamper, Judith Bauer. *New Friends in a New Land.* (Stories of America Series) Steck-Vaughn, 1993. (Grade 2)

Teacher's Resource Binder

Blackline Masters for Unit 2: Unit 2 Project Organizer, Unit 2 Review, Unit 2 Test; Activities for Chapters 3, 4; Outline Map of the World

Chapter Summary American Indians were the first people to live in America. They lived in all parts of what is now the United States. They had different kinds of shelter, clothing, and food, depending on the area in which they lived. Some American Indians hunted buffalo. They used the hides for clothing and to cover their tepees. Other American Indian groups farmed.

Chapter Objectives Students will learn to

- identify the first people that lived in the United States.

- identify how American Indians obtained food, shelter, and clothing.

- read a chart.

Vocabulary

buffalo, p. 24   chart, p. 26

Vocabulary Activities Make a simple chart on the chalkboard with the following two categories: *Food American Indians Hunted* and *Food American Indians Grew*. Write the word *buffalo* under the heading *Food American Indians Hunted*. Have students name different foods they think American Indians ate. Help students understand which category each food belongs in. Then tell students that they have just helped you make a *chart*. Explain that charts help people organize facts.

Before Reading the Chapter Discuss with students some of the ways in which we learn about the past. Discuss books and photographs, but also include artifacts, letters, and oral history. Have students look at the pictures on pages 24 and 25. Generate a discussion about who these people were and when they lived. Tell students that long ago there were vast herds of buffalo. They roamed the part of the United States known as the Great Plains. Point out the Great Plains on a map of the United States. American Indians who lived on the plains depended on the buffalo for food and for many of the other things they needed.

Teaching Suggestions and Answers
Page 23
Invite students to share any prior knowledge they have of American Indians. Encourage them to contribute the names of various groups, such as Sioux, Cheyenne, or Iroquois. Write the names on the chalkboard and introduce the names of local groups with which you are familiar.

Emphasize to students that American Indians lived in different kinds of homes. American Indians of the northeast, such as the Iroquois, lived in wood houses called long houses. Some groups in the southwest built pueblos—towns built from stones and clay like the one pictured here. Some groups, like the Cheyenne and Sioux, lived in tepees. Ask students to suggest building materials that groups living in their area might have used.

Students should mention that like homes in a neighborhood, the people live near each other and that they probably have places to work and play.

Page 24
You might explain to students that American Indians who hunted the buffalo had to move frequently to follow the animals that were continually migrating across the vast plains. The tepees were perfect adaptations to this life-style, because they were easy to take down, move to a new place, and put up again. Also, there were few trees on the plains, so the American Indians could not build wooden houses. You might point out the dog in the picture that is pulling the sled, or travois. American Indians often used dogs in this way, especially before they obtained horses from the Spanish. **Students should circle a tepee, clothing, and the bundle on the travois.**

Project Tip
Help students carry out the suggestion by directing them to books that contain information about animals that live in your area. You may need to help them understand maps or charts that identify the ranges of these animals so they can see which animals live in their area. Introduce students to books about the American

Indian group that lived in your area so they can learn how these animals were used.

Page 25

Explain that farming was hard work for the American Indians. Their tools were simple: pointed sticks for making holes in which to plant seeds and crude hoes made from stone and wood. If students are familiar with irrigation, you might add that some American Indians had extensive irrigation systems that enabled them to grow crops even in very dry lands. Explain that many American Indians also gathered food such as nuts, berries, mushrooms, and wild fruit that grew near where they lived. **Answers will vary. Students may ask about games children played, the kind of education they received, and how old they were when they were first permitted to hunt.**

Page 26

Review the chart with students and discuss the kinds of information given. Guide students to understand that American Indians who lived long ago had the same needs that we have today—food, clothing, and shelter. Ask them how people today get the food, clothing, and shelter they need. (Most people buy or rent shelter and buy their food and clothing, although some build their own homes, grow their own food, and sew their own clothes.) **Students should respond that American Indians built or made their homes. They should answer that they made all their own clothing.**

Page 27

Around the Globe Call attention to the word *Aztecs*. Explain that it is the name of a particular group of American Indians. You might explain that the Aztecs controlled an area of Mexico from the Atlantic to the Pacific Coast. Their capital city was in the same place where Mexico City is today. Point out the area on the world map on page 103. Explain that when the Spanish came to Mexico, they conquered the Aztecs and destroyed their cities. Read the sample sentences with students. Discuss what each picture represents (a lake, a tree, a road). Point out that this story is easy to read because it is made up of both pictures and words. The Aztecs, however, wrote entirely in pictures. Invite students to

speculate on how difficult it would be to read and write using only pictures. Challenge students to invent their own pictures and share them with the rest of the class. **Students should write short stories that use pictures or symbols to stand for some of the words. Stories will vary.**

Page 28

Chapter Checkup You may want to work through the Chapter Checkup with students.

Answers: 1. were the first Americans **2.** hunting and farming **3.** clothing **4.** wrote with pictures instead of letters
Ask several students to volunteer their ideas. Answers will vary, but students should suggest resources that are common in your area. These might include such things as rocks, trees, and clay.

After Reading the Chapter

Read aloud an American Indian legend or folk tale. Explain to students that legends may be based on actual people or events, but they are not regarded as fact.

Writing

Guide students in writing a class letter to American Indian children who go to school on a reservation. Have students tell a little about themselves and ask the American Indian children to share information about their school and culture.

Art

Have students refer to the Aztec picture-writing exercise on page 27 and create more short stories about the American Indians and how they lived. Students can work alone or with a partner. Have students use crayons, markers, or pictures cut from magazines to add color to their stories.

Chapter Summary American Indians were the only people living in America for a long time. Then Christopher Columbus came to America from Europe. Groups of settlers—the settlers of Jamestown and the Pilgrims—came to America more than 100 years after Columbus. American Indians played an essential role in helping the Europeans survive in the new land.

Chapter Objectives Students will learn to

- identify Christopher Columbus.
- identify parts of Earth on a world map and globe.
- identify the Pilgrims as early settlers in the United States.
- describe the origin of Thanksgiving.

Vocabulary

continent, p. 29   globe, p. 30

Vocabulary Activities Review the list of words that was generated for maps in Chapter 1. After students have looked at a world map, ask them if they can think of other words to add to the list (continent, ocean, country, globe, compass rose, and so on). Remind students to use the glossary to help them understand difficult words.

Before Reading the Chapter Ask students if they can name any of the continents or oceans of the world. Write correct answers on the chalkboard. Point out the world map on page 29. Review reading a map and using a compass rose. Remind students that the world is round, but that a world map is flat so that we can see everything at the same time.

Teaching Suggestions and Answers

Page 29
Tell students that Columbus sailed to America in three ships called the *Niña, Pinta,* and *Santa María.* When he landed on the Bahama Islands he was sure that he had reached a place called the East Indies. That is why he named the

people he found there "Indians." It has the word *India* in it and means "people of India." Guide students in finding and reading the names of each of the seven continents. Then help them find each of the four oceans. **Students should draw an *X* on the Atlantic Ocean and should trace Columbus's route to America. Students should write a *C* on North America.**

Page 30
Make sure students understand that this is a picture of a globe and not the globe itself. Show them a globe and help them understand that they only see one half at a time, which is why there are two pictures of the globe shown here. Call attention to the North Pole and South Pole. Remind students of the cardinal directions. Explain that the North Pole is as far north as you can go on Earth. Likewise, the South Pole is as far south as you can go. **Students should circle North America on the picture of the globe. They should circle Europe. They should underline the name of either the Pacific, Arctic, or Indian ocean.**

Page 31
Explain to students that the Pilgrims knew very little about America before they came here. It was much different from Europe. They prepared as well as they could, bringing with them food and supplies on their ship, the *Mayflower.* Point out England on a map or globe. Then show students where Plymouth is. Tell them it is in present-day Massachusetts. Have students trace the Pilgrims' voyage on the map on page 29. **Answers will vary. Possible answers include showing them where stores, schools, and other neighborhood places are located.**

Page 32
Encourage students to tell how their families celebrate Thanksgiving. Ask how many of them eat turkey, corn, squash, and pumpkin—the same foods that the American Indians and Pilgrims ate on the first Thanksgiving. **Answers may vary. Possible answers are that the American Indians helped the Pilgrims to grow food; they had the first Thanksgiving dinner together.**

Project Tip

Direct students to library resources that will help them learn how the American Indian group they are studying got their food.

Page 33

Did You Know? Explain that the settlers at Jamestown were more interested in finding gold and silver than in farming. The settlement nearly failed because they did not at first devote themselves to building a permanent settlement and learning to farm. They were saved by American Indians who brought food to the starving settlers. Jamestown is located in present-day Virginia. The town has been preserved and looks much as it did long ago. Thousands of people visit Jamestown each year. **Students should answer that Jamestown has houses and gardens and places for people to work, just like neighborhoods today.**

Page 34

Special People Inform students that Pocahontas was the daughter of the chief of the Powhatan, the group of American Indians living near the Jamestown settlement. Her name means "playful one." Pocahontas married one of the Jamestown settlers, John Rolfe, and returned to London with her husband. In London society she was known as Lady Rebecca Rolfe. She became ill and died before she could return home. Remind students that the colonists and American Indians did not speak the same language. Encourage students to speculate on the misunderstandings that could arise in such a situation. **Answers will vary. Possible answers: show or demonstrate activities; draw pictures; find someone who speaks her language who can translate for you.**

Page 35

Chapter Checkup You may want to work through the Chapter Checkup with students. Make sure they all understand what the correct answers are to the numbered questions.

Answers: 1. Earth **2.** continent **3.** Atlantic **4.** Thanksgiving
Invite students to share their ideas with the class. Answers might include that both groups of people were from England; both groups had to learn to hunt, fish, and plant crops; both groups were helped by American Indians.

After Reading the Chapter

Have students role-play the first meeting between the English settlers of Plymouth and the American Indians of the area. Allow them time to plan the skit. Urge them to think about questions the two groups might want to ask one another and the information they would want to share. Remind students that the Pilgrims and American Indians did not speak the same language.

Writing

Ask students to imagine they are Christopher Columbus or Pocahontas. Encourage them to write a diary entry about one of the events in the life of either Christopher Columbus or Pocahontas.

Drama

Challenge students to plan a skit based on the Pilgrims during their voyage to America. Have students include the discomfort of the trip, the hunger and fear, and the hopes and dreams for a new life.

Writing

Remind students that when the Pilgrims came to America, they were entering a vast wilderness that required special survival skills. Tell students that people who plan a wilderness camping trip must have the same kind of skills. Ask students to write a plan for such a trip. Have them describe the supplies and equipment (food, special clothing, tents, water) and skills they will need (fire building, reading a compass, pitching a tent).

Design/Architecture

Have students work in small groups. Ask them to imagine themselves as early settlers in our country. Have them design a settlement. They can make a drawing of the settlement, labeling the various structures, and then can draw or paint scenes of daily life to accompany their design plans.

Unit Summary The people in neighborhoods work at many jobs. Some people also do volunteer work. All of them provide the goods and services that people need and want. Our needs and wants determine how we spend our income. A budget and savings help us plan what to buy. People pay taxes to their community to pay for the services and other things that make the community a pleasant, safe place to live.

Before Reading the Unit Ask each student to name the job of an adult he or she knows. List the jobs on the chalkboard. Discuss with students the variety of jobs and why each is important. Ask them why they think people choose the jobs they do. Next, tell students to look at the picture on page 38, and ask them to notice the clothes the workers are wearing and the items they are holding. Ask students to guess some of the jobs the people in the photo have. Lead a discussion about the special clothing people wear for certain jobs. Have students think of some jobs that require uniforms (police officer, mail carrier, basketball player). Point out also that although some workers don't wear uniforms, they wear special clothing to keep them safe. For example, construction workers and some factory workers wear hard hats and steel-toed boots. Then direct students' attention to the questions. Have students look at the Unit Project box. Discuss the project, and explain that Project Tips in each chapter will help them see how the project relates to the content of the chapter.

Unit Project

Setting Up the Project Lead a brainstorming session to come up with questions students might ask of workers. Then divide the class into teams to plan a strategy for locating and talking to workers. Urge teams to include service workers, workers who make goods, and volunteers.

Students will find specific suggestions in the Project Tip sections of the chapters. Encourage them to adapt the suggestions to their own interests.

Presenting the Project As an alternative to the suggested unit project, you might suggest that students write and illustrate a book about jobs. Each student could write a description and draw pictures of one job. The descriptions and pictures can be assembled into a book that other students can read.

After Reading the Unit Direct students to look back at the unit opener questions and to discuss the answers. Encourage additional discussion by asking: Do all people work for the same reason? Do all people have the same needs and wants? Do all people spend their income in the same way?

Skill Builder

Using a Picture Graph

Remind students that picture graphs make information easy and quick to understand. Call students' attention to the picture graph on page 61, and tell them to look at the line with the most pictures. Stress that they can tell at a glance that there are more judges than school bus drivers.

Answers: 1. 6 judges **2.** 4 school bus drivers **3.** Students should draw 6 trees on the chart to represent city park workers. **4.** Answers will vary. Possible answers: numbers of girls and boys, numbers of teachers and pupils, numbers of second graders and first graders.

Bibliography

Teacher

Marcello, Jody Smothers. *The World Book Encyclopedia of People and Places.* World Book, Inc., 1992.

McClintock, Joack. *Everything Is Somewhere: The Geography Quiz Book.* Quill, 1986.

Natoli, S. (ed.). *Strengthening Geography in the Social Studies.* National Council for the Social Studies, 1992.

Student

Bailey, Donna. *Farmers.* (Facts About Series) Macmillan Publishers, Ltd., 1989. (Grades 2–3)

Humphrey, Paul. *People at Work.* (Read All About It Series) Steck-Vaughn, 1995. (Grade 2)

Kanetzke, Howard W. *Trains and Railroads.* Steck-Vaughn, 1991. (Grade 2)

Teacher's Resource Binder

Blackline Masters for Unit 3: Unit 3 Project Organizer, Unit 3 Review, Unit 3 Test; Activities for Chapters 5, 6, 7

Chapter Summary People work to produce goods and services that people need and want. A community such as a town or city may be composed of many neighborhoods. People in a community have many jobs. Some of them work to produce goods. Others provide services. Among the service workers, some, like firefighters and police officers, provide community services. Others, such as attorneys, cooks, and doctors, provide commercial services.

Chapter Objectives Students will learn to

• identify and define needs and wants.

• identify and distinguish between goods and services.

• read and use a picture graph.

Vocabulary	
needs, p. 39	community, p. 40
wants, p. 39	goods, p. 40
picture graph, p. 39	services, p. 42

Vocabulary Activities Make two copies for each student of the Concept Web graphic organizer found on page 48 of this guide. Tell students they will be using the webs to help them understand some of the vocabulary terms in this chapter. Reproduce the Concept Web on the chalkboard to show students how to use the web. At the center of the first of the webs, students should write the world *needs*. At the center of the other web, they should write *wants*. As students read, have them decide if an item is a "need" or a "want," and write it in the appropriate web. Students may add other items from their own lives. The exercise could be expanded with a web for "goods" and a web for "services." For students who have difficulty with any of these vocabulary terms, help them use the glossary to review the terms.

Before Reading the Chapter Ask students what jobs they see their neighbors doing each day. Discuss any major industry that is located in your neighborhood. Discuss why these various industries are important to the community. Ask students if they have ever needed to work with someone else to get a job done. Have students describe what it was like.

Teaching Suggestions and Answers
Page 39
Be sure that students have a clear understanding of the differences between needs and wants. Give an example such as a snack food and milk. Emphasize that the snack food is a want because it is not necessary for health, while milk is a necessity because it helps our bodies remain healthy by building strong teeth and bones. Have students look at the picture graph. Read the labels with students and help them understand how to read it across from the left to the right columns. **Students should color the five balls. They should draw three kites on line 2. They should draw one hat on line 3.** Emphasize that a picture graph helps readers understand facts easily and quickly. Illustrate by asking, which item do the fewest children want? (hat) Which item do the most children want? (ball)

Page 40
Write the name of your community on the chalkboard. Guide students in understanding that many neighborhoods make up the community. Stress that goods are things that are made. Tell students to look around the room. Point out that most of the objects they see are goods. **Students should put a *P* over the picture on the left of the worker making the part for the toy. Students should put a *B* over the picture on the right of the worker putting the toy in a box.**

Page 41
Discuss why people work together. Point out that often a job is too big for one person and that it is quicker if more people help. Suggest that it is sometimes more fun when people work together. Ask students about their experiences working with other people. **Students should circle the machines workers are using.**

Page 42
Stress that services are not things but work that is done to help someone. Sometimes people

receive both goods and services when they buy something. When you buy a pair of shoes, you get a good—the shoes—plus the service of the person selling and fitting the shoes. **For photograph 1, students should write: help sick people and keep people well. For photograph 2, students should write: put out fires.**

Page 43

Explain to students that some people who provide services, such as dentists and hairdressers, are paid by their customers. Others, such as police officers and teachers, are paid by the community. Have students name the jobs done by the workers shown in the two photographs on page 43 (chef, television camera operator). Point out that although both workers are providing a service, the chef provides a good in the food that he prepares, and the camera operator provides a good in the finished film he makes. **Students should write the names of two service jobs.**

Project Tip
Discuss the tip with students. Help students list and categorize jobs. You might have them tally service and manufacturing jobs to see what kinds of jobs most people they know do.

Page 44

Technology Ask students to pretend they are going on a picnic. How will they get the food to the picnic? (Carry it in a picnic basket, shopping bag, or cooler) What special care is needed for some of the food? (Juice or soup needs to be kept in an insulated container; sandwiches must be wrapped in plastic wrap or aluminum foil; salads need to be kept cool.) Help students see the correlation between their imaginary picnic and moving large volumes of food or goods from the farm or manufacturer to the store. **Students should respond that ice cream is moved in a special truck. It must be kept very cold so it will not melt.**

Page 45

Around the Globe Use a world map or globe to point out Brazil, South America, Sri Lanka, and Asia. Tell students that Brazil grows more bananas than any other country. Explain that bananas can grow in some parts of the United States, such as Texas and Florida, but that we do not grow them in great numbers. Explain that natural rubber comes from the juice of a rubber tree. These trees grow in places where the weather is hot and moist, such as Sri Lanka. All rubber goods are not made from natural rubber, however. Some are made from synthetic rubber, which is made from chemicals. Synthetic rubber is made in many places around the world. **Students should list goods made of rubber. Items will vary but may include the following: erasers, balls, tires, shoe soles, rubber bands.**

Page 46

Chapter Checkup Make sure all students understand what the correct answers are to the numbered questions.

Answers: 1. community **2.** needs **3.** goods **4.** service
Students should answer that the workers pictured give us services.

After Reading the Chapter

Have students make a job collage by drawing or cutting out pictures of people doing various jobs.

Writing
Have students write a class letter to your local fire station, thanking the firefighters for the services they provide. If possible, arrange for a tour of the station. Alternatively, a firefighter might be asked to visit your classroom and talk with students.

Civics
Discuss reasons why volunteering is important to the community. Have students list volunteer projects they have done or would like to do. Then, challenge them to organize a clean-up or a recycling program for your classroom or school.

Writing
Have students think of someone they admire, such as the President, an actor, a sports figure, or an astronaut. Have them write a letter to the person telling what they admire about the person and asking questions about their job.

Chapter Summary Some people choose jobs because they enjoy them. Others choose jobs because they like to help people. Sometimes, people choose jobs because they live in an area where certain special jobs exist, such as jobs on boats or in resort towns. Children also have jobs they do at school and at home.

Chapter Objectives Students will learn to

- identify some of the job choices people have and make.

- recognize how climate and geography can affect job opportunities and choices.

Vocabulary

volunteers, p. 51   slave, p. 51

Vocabulary Activities Ask students if they have ever heard the word *volunteer*. Have students share their understandings of the word. Point out to students that when people are forced to do work for no pay, they are called *slaves*, not volunteers. Direct any students who are having trouble with the terms to consult the glossary.

Before Reading the Chapter Have students look through the photographs in the chapter and identify as many different occupations as they can. Ask students to think of all the jobs they might like to do as adults. Follow-up questions might include: What kind of training do these jobs require? Do you know any people now who do these jobs? Ask students if there is a particular location where they would like to live. Have them think about the types of jobs they could do there. Then ask them to think of jobs that could *not* be done there.

Teaching Suggestions and Answers
Page 47
Point out to students that most people have jobs because they must earn money to buy the things they need and want. Emphasize that people also try to find jobs they enjoy. Often they look for jobs that allow them to do things they enjoy doing anyway. Teachers enjoy being with people. They enjoy helping students to learn. Baseball players like playing baseball. Mechanics like working on cars. **Answers will vary. They should name a job they would like to do and then draw a picture of themselves doing it.**

Page 48
Point out to students that we need people to do certain jobs. Invite students to list jobs they or the community need to have done. (Possible answers: nurses, doctors, street workers, police officers, firefighters, teachers, trash collectors.) Tell students that people often go to school or take special courses to get training for jobs they want. Ask them to think about skills needed for certain jobs. What kind of skill does a newspaper reporter need? (writing ability) What skills does a doctor need? (knowledge of how to treat different illnesses) **Answers will vary. Possible answers include: cleaning the school, the custodian; cooking the lunch, the cook; helping students safely cross streets, the crossing guard; transporting students to and from school, bus drivers.**

Project Tip
Help students carry out the suggestion on page 48. Encourage students to talk to workers they see at the school, to neighbors or friends they know, or to certain workers in the community such as firefighters, postal workers, or police officers. Caution them against speaking with anyone they do not know.

Page 49
Discuss the kinds of jobs that are suitable for certain kinds of places. Flat lands, for example, are often suited to farming. Many jobs in these areas involve farming, farm equipment sales and repair, animal care, and truck driving. There are many ski resorts in the mountains. People have jobs clearing roads of snow, teaching vacationers to ski, cooking and serving food, and working on the ski slopes. Discuss the photographs. Guide students in identifying the jobs being done. **For picture 1, students should circle *unloading fish*; for picture 2, they should circle *moving snow*.** Discuss the climate and type of land where your school is located. Guide students in discussing jobs that are well-suited to your area and those that are not.

Page 50

Ask students to name some of the jobs that need to be done in the classroom each day. (Handing out work, sharpening pencils, erasing the chalkboard) **Students should circle the picture of the teacher and each of the students.** Invite students to talk about jobs they do at home. **Students should write one job they do. Answers might include washing dishes, walking the dog, taking out the trash.**

Page 51

Special People You might want to tell students briefly about slavery in the United States. Explain that long ago, people were kept as slaves in many states in the South. Some of these people ran away to the states in the North and to Canada where they could be free. On a United States map, show students the states in the South and North and Canada. Tell students a war was fought that ended slavery in the United States. Explain to students that, because Harriet Tubman believed slavery was wrong, she risked her life to become a leader of the Underground Railroad. The Underground Railroad was a system that helped slaves escape. It was called "underground" because it was secret. It was called a railroad because there were regular routes that slaves followed in reaching freedom. People along the way provided runaway slaves with food and places to hide as they traveled North. These places were called "stations." Discuss volunteer work with students. Ask students to name some jobs that volunteers do in their community (picking up litter, visiting people in the hospital, helping the homeless, tutoring students, leading scouting groups, organizing disaster relief). Invite students to speculate why some people decide to work for free. Guide students to understand that people do it because they enjoy the work, want to help others, or believe some work is so important that it must be done. **Answers will vary, but students should list jobs that help others.**

Page 52

Chapter Checkup Make sure all students understand what the correct answers are to the numbered questions.

Answers: 1. F **2.** T **3.** T **4.** T

Encourage students to tell what jobs they would like to do and why. Answers will vary but students should name a job that will help the neighborhood, and they should tell why they would want to do the job.

After Reading the Chapter

Arrange for some parents of your students to visit the class and discuss their jobs and the training these jobs require. Some parents may have had on-the-job training. Others may still be going to school. Prepare students by leading them in a brainstorming session to list questions they can ask during the presentations.

Writing

Have students write a class letter to another second-grade class at a school in a different part of the country. Have students ask students in the other class about their career interests. Have students compare career interests to see if the area and climate where people live has an effect on their career choices.

Social Studies

Discuss with students some work they could volunteer to do as a class that would help people who live in the neighborhood or community. Help students think of ideas by suggesting that they could pick up litter in a park or beach area or help teach something to a younger class or group of children. Encourage students to think of other volunteer work they could do. If possible, help students follow through with their ideas.

Chapter Summary People cannot buy everything, so they must choose how to spend their income. They make a budget to help decide how to spend money, and they keep savings in order to purchase more expensive things. People pay taxes to the community so the community can pay for the services it provides.

Chapter Objectives Students will learn to

- identify and define *income, budget,* and *savings.*

- explain how a budget helps them buy things they need and want.

- identify how taxes are collected and how the money is used.

Vocabulary	
income, p. 53	savings, p. 56
budget, p. 54	taxes, p. 57

Vocabulary Activities Create with students a classroom bulletin-board display about money. Some students may draw pictures of the various United States coins and bills. They can pin them on the board. Other students may draw or cut pictures out of magazines that show things we buy with money. Others may add pictures of the items we buy with our savings. Each group of items should be labeled. As students read the chapter, add the vocabulary term *taxes* to the bulletin board. Have students draw pictures of things tax money pays for and add those pictures to the display. Help students who have difficulty with the terms use the glossary.

Before Reading the Chapter On the chalkboard, write a short grocery list, and have students guess how much they think each item costs. Write down their responses. Then write down the actual cost of each item. Discuss why it is important to plan how much money you spend and what you spend it on. If students get an allowance, ask volunteers to discuss what they do with their money. Ask if any students put money in a savings account. Invite students to explain why they think people save money.

Teaching Suggestions and Answers
Page 53
Ask students to name ways in which they could earn an income. Possibilities include receiving an allowance for doing household chores or walking a dog. Invite students to tell what they do when they cannot have everything they want. Guide students to the conclusion that they make choices. **Students should write an *N* on the man purchasing vegetables. They should write a *W* on the woman buying jewelry.**

Page 54
Ask students what could happen to the García family if they do not make a budget. Point out that the Garcías might run out of money and not be able to pay for some things they need or that they want. **Students should put an *X* next to these questions: How much will the trip cost? How much income do we have?** Tell students that long ago people did not use money. Instead, they traded goods or services they had for the goods and services they wanted. Ask students if they ever trade for things they want. Then encourage them to speculate on whether they think this is a good way to do things. Ask them if they think it would be easy to work out trades for everything that a family needs and wants.

Page 55
Answers will vary, but student choices should not add up to more than $5.00. Discuss the different choices students make. Demonstrate that there is only enough money for certain items. Invite volunteers to discuss real-life choices they have had to make in spending their allowances.

Project Tip
Discuss the tip with students, and help them understand how the suggestion connects to the main ideas of this chapter. Explain that people work because they want or need something, but sometimes what they need and want is not income. Sometimes they want to help people or make the neighborhood a better place to live. They may be happy to volunteer their time to get these things. You might lead the class in brainstorming a list of volunteer jobs that

children can do and another list of volunteer jobs in the community.

Page 56

Tell students that when savings are put in a bank, the money can earn more money, or interest, just by being in the bank. Explain that the bank not only keeps the money safe, it also uses the money to loan to other people. The bank pays the interest in exchange for the right to use the money it is keeping. Explain the use of checks to students. Emphasize that people use checks like money, but people can write a check only if they have money in the bank to cover it. **Students should draw a picture of something they want that they would like to save money for.**

Page 57

Explain to students that people pay taxes in many ways. They pay income taxes on money they earn, they pay sales tax on things they buy, and they pay property tax on their home. Explain how children pay sales taxes when they buy things they want. Ask students to identify some community services that are paid for with taxes. (Possible answers: paying public school staff members, cleaning and repairing streets, caring for parks and playgrounds, fighting fires, keeping the community safe.) Ask students to speculate on what the community would be like without these services. **Students should respond that the teacher helps them learn, the police officer keeps them safe, and the librarian helps them find books and use other library resources.**

Page 58

Ask students to think about other services that their community pays for with tax money. Who pays to have your public schools built? If applicable, ask who pays for the salt or sand used to keep snowy, icy streets safe. **Students should respond that if the hole is not fixed, cars could get damaged and people might be hurt.**

Page 59

Technology Tell students that the United States government makes five different coins. They are the penny, nickel, dime, quarter, and half dollar. The government also makes six different bills: $1, $5, $10, $20, $50, and $100. Until recently, the government also made a one-dollar coin and a $2 bill. Some of these coins and bills are still in circulation and are legal tender. Explain that one-dollar bills usually wear out after about one and a half years. Banks then collect these bills and send them to the Federal Reserve Bank where the old bills are replaced by new bills. The old ones are then shredded. Ask students why they think the old bills are shredded. (So they cannot be used again) **Students should draw a picture of a bill that they would design.**

Page 60

Chapter Checkup Make sure students understand what the correct answers are to the numbered questions.

Answers: 1. to help them plan how to spend their money **2.** to buy things we want that cost a lot of money **3.** They use the money they get from taxes.
Invite several students to share their answers with the class. Possible answers include that schools and roads would not get fixed; new schools and roads would not be built; service workers would not get paid.

After Reading the Chapter

Set up a bank in your classroom. Students can use tokens or play money. Give students an "income" for work done in the classroom. Have students make their own bank books, and keep track of their deposits and withdrawals over a specific period of time.

Writing

Have students think of a community worker they have observed. Ask them to write a description of the job, telling two or three things the worker does.

Unit Summary People make rules and laws to keep our schools and communities safe, clean, and fair. Rules and laws can be changed or replaced when the need arises. Community leaders, such as the mayor, governor, and President, are elected to help make the new rules and laws and to see that those rules and laws are obeyed. Many problems can be solved without making new laws, however, when people work together.

Before Reading the Unit Ask students what rules and laws they follow each day. (Possible answers: making their beds, brushing their teeth, going to school, listening to the teacher, and obeying the school crossing guard.) Then have students read the unit opener on page 63 and look at the photograph. Ask them to tell what rules and laws the photo shows. Ask students to name who has to obey the crossing guard. Guide students in understanding that both pedestrians and drivers must pay attention to the crossing guard. Ask a student to read the questions aloud. Tell students to look for answers to these questions as they read the unit. Next, read and discuss the project described in the Unit Project box and remind students to look for Project Tips in each chapter.

Unit Project

Setting Up the Project Have students brainstorm a few problems at their school. Discuss some of the problems to help students identify the kinds they should name. Encourage teams to continue to observe and to think about problems in school as they go about their routines for a few days. Students will find specific suggestions in the Project Tip sections of the chapters. Encourage them to adapt the suggestions to their own interests.

Presenting the Project Students can use the suggestions appearing on page 85 or think of another way to present their project. You might suggest that teams work together and take on the role of a legislative body. Each team can present its rule and give a speech explaining the need for it. The class can then vote for or against it.

After Reading the Unit Have students review the questions in the unit opener and discuss their answers. Prompt further discussion by asking

such questions as: How do rules and laws help people get along? What would happen if we did not have rules and laws? Why do people sometimes try to solve problems without making new laws? Do laws always stay the same or can laws change?

Skill Builder

Reading a Map of the United States

Remind students that they can read a map if they know what the symbols and compass rose mean. Help students interpret the map key.

Answers: 1. Students should circle Washington, D.C., on the map. **2.** Students should color any three states on the east coast red. **3.** Students should color any three of the states bordering the Pacific blue. **4.** Students should write an *N* on the north part of Alaska on the inset map.

Bibliography

Teacher

Huff, Barbara A. *Greening the City Streets: The Story of Community Gardens.* Clarion Books, 1990.

Nelson, Nigel. *Signs and Symbols.* Thomson Learning, 1993.

Posey-Pacak, Melissa L. *Earth at Risk.* NCGE, 1991.

Student

Amos, Janine. *Pollution.* (First Starts Series) Steck-Vaughn, 1993. (Grades 1–2)

Herschell, Michael. *Animals in Danger.* (Read All About It Series) Steck-Vaughn, 1995. (Grade 2)

Humphrey, Paul, and Alex Ramsay. *Look Out on the Road.* (Read All About It Series) Steck-Vaughn, 1995. (Grade 2)

Ramsay, Helena. *Safety at Home.* (Read All About It Series) Steck-Vaughn, 1995. (Grade 2)

Riley, Gail Blasser. *Who Will Help?* (Steppingstone Stories Series) Steck-Vaughn, 1991. (Grades K–2)

Teacher's Resource Binder

Blackline Masters for Unit 4: Unit 4 Project Organizer, Unit 4 Review, Unit 4 Test; Activities for Chapters 8, 9, 10; Outline Map of the United States

Chapter Summary People make rules and laws to keep people and the places where we live and work safe, and to keep things fair. Laws are written rules that communities make in order to help people live together.

Chapter Objectives Students will learn to

- identify what rules are and why they are important.

- identify laws and see why they are made.

- explain why we follow rules and laws.

Vocabulary

rules, p. 64   laws, p. 66

Vocabulary Activities Make two columns on the chalkboard. Label one column "rules" and the other column "laws." Have students add examples to each column. As students read, have them identify the rules and laws, and tell where to write them on the chalkboard.

Before Reading the Chapter Review with students some of the rules used at school, such as *no loud talking* and *no running in the halls.* Have students consider the reasons for each rule. Ask students to name a rule about crossing the street. Ask students to think of a rule about watching television. Discuss with students why these rules are important and what might happen if they are not followed. Have students think of reasons for their rules.

Teaching Suggestions and Answers
Page 64
Students should write one rule they follow at school. Ask students to tell what rule they wrote and then to explain the reason for the rule. Ask students who makes the rules. Do they apply to everyone? Ask students to name some other places besides school where they follow rules. (Community library, playground, park, home) Have students name some rules they follow at home. Ask them to explain the reasons for the rules.

Page 65
Discuss each picture with students. Make sure they understand that in the picture on the left the child turned the wrong way is fooling around. In the picture on the right they should understand that there are other people waiting to bat the ball. Ask students how they feel when they see someone breaking the rules. Invite students to give examples and to tell what they said or did. Discuss what children should do when someone does not follow the rules at school, at home, or in the neighborhood. Ask students to name who makes rules. (parents, teachers and principals, other groups of people) Ask students if they have ever made rules. If so, invite them to tell what rules they made and why they needed them. Ask students to tell what happened when someone did not follow the rules. **Students should draw a line matching the illustration with the rule that describes it. Students should circle the child who is fooling around in line. Possible reasons why it is important to follow this rule include the following: people might get hurt if the rule is not followed, and not following the rule is unfair to others.**

Page 66
Explain that laws are rules that are made by the government to keep people safe and to help make things fair. Discuss with students why communities need traffic signals. Ask students: In which picture is the light red? Green? Yellow? What does a yellow light tell a car driver to do? (slow down) What does a red light tell a car driver to do? (stop) **Students should respond that the green light means "go." They should write the name of one community law, such as a traffic or litter law.**

Page 67
Discuss the three pictures on the page to make sure students understand what is happening in each one. Then discuss what the laws listed on the page mean and why they are important. **Students should number the illustration of the police officer and car *1*; the boy throwing litter on the street *3*; the woman walking her dog *2*. Students should put a checkmark next to the**

illustration of the woman walking her dog. Ask students to think of some other laws that people obey. (Answers may include wearing safety belts, paying taxes, and going to school.) Ask students what can happen to people who break the law. (They may be fined or sent to jail.) Discuss the differences between a law and a rule. Explain that rules are made by parents, teachers, and other groups of people; laws are made by the government. Discuss the role of police officers in enforcing the community's laws.

Project Tip

Discuss the Project Tip with students. Help them understand that recognizing and solving a problem in school relates to the topic of rules that they are studying in this chapter. Encourage students to write down all the problems that they can think of, even if they do not see how the problem can be solved. Someone else on their team may have an idea that will help fix it.

Page 68

Did You Know? Discuss what each of the signs mean. Ask students which ones they see in their community. Invite students to tell about other signs outside of school and around their community that remind them of rules or laws. **Students should make a sign that shows one rule in their neighborhood or school.**

Page 69

Chapter Checkup You may want to work through the Chapter Checkup with students. Make sure they all understand what the correct answers are to the numbered questions.

Answers: **1.** Rules and laws help people live together. **2.** Do not make loud noises at night that may bother people. **3.** to keep people safe Students should name a rule or law they obeyed today and explain how it helps people live together.

After Reading the Chapter

Discuss with students what would happen if they lived in a neighborhood that had no rules or laws. What would traffic be like? Would the neighborhood be noisy? As you discuss the situation with students, have them generate a list of rules and laws that would restore peace and make things safe and fair.

Art

Students can choose a playground where children need to follow safety rules. Have students list safety rules on posterboard and then add drawings to illustrate how the rules are good for people. Invite them to post the rules at the playground.

Civics

Have students pretend to be mayor of your city. Ask them to think of three things they would like to do to improve the city. Students should also tell three things they like about the city.

Writing

Tell students to imagine that a class of second-grade students in another country has written them a letter. They want to know about going to school in the United States and about the rules American schoolchildren must obey. Have students write a letter in response, telling about some important rules and explaining the purpose behind them.

Social Studies

Tell groups of students to imagine they have been chosen to make a sign for an international airport. Explain to students that many of the people using the airport might not speak or read English, so the signs must tell about a rule through pictures and symbols. Rules students might illustrate include: No littering, No exit, No smoking, No pets.

History

Have students look back at the pictures of the Pilgrims and the Jamestown settlement on pages 31–33 of the text. Then ask students to imagine that they were among the settlers of Jamestown. Ask students to write three rules they think would have been important to have in the settlement.

Chapter Summary Rules and laws are made and changed. The people of a community elect leaders by voting for them. The Mayors lead communities, governors lead states, and the President leads the country. Each state has a capital city where the governor and state leaders work. The capital of the United States is Washington, D.C.

Chapter Objectives Students will learn to

- identify reasons why laws are created or changed.
- identify leaders (mayor, governor, President).
- explain how a leader is selected.
- read a map of the United States.

Vocabulary

leaders, p. 70	insets, p. 72
government, p. 70	governor, p. 73
mayor, p. 71	President, p. 73
vote, p. 71	capital, p. 74
state, p. 72	

Vocabulary Activities Make a word web with the word *leaders* at the center. You may want to use the Concept Web graphic organizer found on page 48 of this guide for this purpose. Add the words *mayor, governor,* and *President* to the spokes. Discuss with students the different roles these leaders play in government. Help students who have trouble with the vocabulary terms use the glossary.

Before Reading the Chapter Ask students if they have ever voted for something or someone. Invite students to tell about the experience. Ask them how they made their decision. Do they think that voting is a good way to choose leaders and to make laws and rules?

Teaching Suggestions and Answers
Page 70
Explain that sometimes people vote directly to change a law or to make a new one. For example, people in some communities have

voted to recycle trash in their neighborhoods. **Students should write one law they would like to change.** Invite students to tell what law they named and to explain why they think it should be changed.

Page 71
Ask students who they think should be allowed to vote for community leaders. Explain that in the United States, men and women who are at least 18 years old are allowed to vote. Tell students that long ago, women, African Americans, and some other groups were not allowed to vote. It took many years, but finally the laws were changed to make it fair and to allow all adults to vote. Invite students to speculate why people under 18 are not allowed to vote. **Students should write the name of their community leader and write a question that they would like the leader to answer.**

Project Tip
Discuss the Project Tip on page 71. Encourage students to explain the problem to adult family members as well as to other adults and students in the school. Remind them to list the ideas that these people give them.

Page 72
Explain to students that the inset maps of Alaska and Hawaii do not show where these states are really located. Show students the actual location of these states on a map of North America. Help students find their own state on the map. You may want to write the state name on the chalkboard so students can see how it is spelled. **They should circle the name on the map. They should underline the names of each of the states that border their state.** Review the use of a compass rose and help students identify states or oceans that are in each of the cardinal directions.

Page 73
Write the name of your town's leader, your state's governor, and that of the President of the United States on the chalkboard. Tell students the title of your town leader—mayor or city manager, for example. Ask students if they know the name of the first President of the

United States (George Washington) or the names of other Presidents. Record the names on the chalkboard, and invite students to share what they know about these leaders. **Students should write the town leader's, governor's, and the President's names.**

Page 74

Ask students if they know the name of their state capital. Write the name on the chalkboard. You might show them where it is located on a state or United States map. Have students turn back to the United States map on page 72. Tell them to look at the map key and then find the capital of the United States on the map. **Students should write the name of their state capital.**

Page 75

Special People Explain that Frederick Douglass was born a slave in the state of Maryland. When he was about twenty years old, he escaped to the state of Massachusetts, where slavery was not permitted. Help students find Maryland and Massachusetts on the United States map on page 72. Douglass began speaking out against slavery and soon became famous in Europe and across the United States. He spoke to President Lincoln about the problem many times. He was an eloquent speaker and became a very educated man. He later held several important positions in the United States government. Ask students if they can name someone else that they have read about who helped end slavery. (Harriet Tubman) **Answers will vary, but students might respond that they could write a letter or speak to a community leader who can help change the law.**

Page 76

Chapter Checkup Make sure all students understand what the correct answers are to the numbered questions.

Answers: 1. leaders **2.** vote **3.** governor
4. President
Ask students to share their answers with the class. Many may suggest that good leaders are important because they help make good laws and get rid of bad ones. Others may respond that good leaders are needed because they help make the community a good place to live.

After Reading the Chapter

If you do not already have a class President and/or Vice President, this is a good time to hold a class election. Have students vote by secret ballot. Have a committee count the votes.

Writing

Have students think of something that is unfair or something they would like changed in their school. Have them write a class letter to the principal explaining their position and asking him or her to help bring about change.

Civics

Ask students to think of a place in their neighborhood that needs improvement. Have students write a class letter to the mayor suggesting what needs to be done.

Reading

Check your library for age-appropriate biographies of leaders such as Abraham Lincoln, Theodore Roosevelt, Susan B. Anthony, and Dr. Martin Luther King, Jr., who were influential in bringing about changes in the laws of our country. Have interested students read about one of these leaders and prepare a written or oral report.

Chapter Summary Laws are not always needed to solve community problems. Some problems such as littering and pollution can be reduced by people working together.

Chapter Objectives Students will learn to

- identify ways to solve problems without making new laws.

- identify the use of signs to remind us of existing laws.

- recognize the need to clean up and prevent pollution.

Vocabulary

pollution, p. 81

Vocabulary Activities Build a word web with students for types of pollution. You may want to use the Concept Web graphic organizer on page 48 of this guide for this purpose. At the center of the web, write *pollution.* Make sure that students understand the meaning of this word (anything that dirties the air, water, or land). Have students generate a list of things that are polluted or that make pollution. As students read and look at the pictures, have them add the information to the web.

Before Reading the Chapter Ask if students have ever tried or worked with others (family, neighbors) to find a solution to a problem, whether big or small. Ask volunteers to share their experiences with the class.

Teaching Suggestions and Answers

Page 77

Point out to students that most communities have laws about making noise that disturbs neighbors. Mr. Barker does not want to call the police. He wants to find another solution to the problem. Help students define the problem by asking: What does Mr. Barker need? (peace and quiet so he can sleep) What do the children need? (to be able to play) **Students should write their solutions to the problem. Answers may**

include talking to the children, sleeping in a different place, finding another place for the children to play.

Page 78

Ask students if they think the plan to clean up the field is a good solution to the problem. Why or why not? (Answers may include yes, because it will give the children a place to play where they won't disturb Mr. Barker, or no, because it will be too hard to clean up.) **Students should describe what needs to be done to clean up the field: The grass must be cut; the paper, cans, and other trash must be picked up.** Discuss these questions with students: Where do you play after school? Do you think about whether you are disturbing neighbors? Where else could you play?

Page 79

Ask students to look at the picture. Ask them who is helping to clean up the field. (all the neighbors) Discuss the concept of cooperation, helping students understand that this solution works because everyone accepts the solution and works together to get the job done. Ask students what someone in the neighborhood should do if he or she thinks there is a better solution. Guide students to understand that alternative solutions should be discussed with the neighbors. Emphasize that sometimes people need to cooperate even though they don't entirely agree with a solution. Problems cannot be solved by continuing to disagree. **Students should circle** *digging, picking up cans and paper,* **and** *raking the grass.*

Page 80

Review signs with students, telling them that signs remind us what to do and what not to do. Ask students what kinds of signs they have seen in parks and playgrounds. Then point out that Mr. Barker and the neighbors made rules about keeping the park clean and they used signs to remind people. Emphasize that following the rules is a way of cooperating with neighbors and working together to solve a problem (how to keep the park clean). **Students should draw a picture of something they can do to make their community better.**

Project Tip

Discuss the Project Tip with students. Point out that Mr. Barker and his neighbors used rules to help keep the park clean when they finished. Emphasize that the rules only work if people obey them. Encourage students to think about rules that people will agree with and obey to solve their unit project problem.

Page 81

Create a chart on the chalkboard with three columns labeled *land, water,* and *air.* Have students give examples of each kind of pollution in their community or in other places. Discuss the causes of some of the pollution and invite students to speculate about solutions. Have students look at the photograph. Discuss the source of the pollution. Tell students that although the kind of pollution emitted from the smokestacks of factories is highly visible, other less obvious sources of air pollution are also very serious. Cars, trucks, ships, and planes are the leading sources of air pollution in the United States. The fuel used to heat and cool buildings is also a major cause of air pollution. Tell students that the government has passed laws designed to control pollution, but that laws cannot solve the problem completely. Ask students what people can do as individuals to cut down on the amount of pollution caused by cars and trucks (drive less, join car pools).

Page 82

Around the Globe Explain to students that there are many animals in danger of disappearing from Earth. Some of these animals are in the United States. These include the bald eagle, grizzly bear, Florida panther, and red wolf. Among those animals endangered in other parts of the world are the giant panda, mountain gorilla, tiger, cheetah, elephant, Asian lion, and black rhinoceros. Explain that most endangered animals are threatened because the places they live are being changed and used by people in ways that do not allow the animals to live there. Emphasize that unless people work together to make room on Earth for these animals, the animals will disappear forever. **Students should create a poster reminding people that they must work together to protect the endangered animals of the world.**

Page 83

Chapter Checkup Make sure all students understand what the correct answers are to the numbered questions.

Answers: 1. F **2.** T **3.** T **4.** F
Encourage students to share their ideas. Possible answers: put up signs, get trash cans.

After Reading the Chapter

Have students work in small groups to role-play solving a problem such as where to go on a field trip or what to serve for lunch. Tell students that the group must work together to reach an agreement.

Art

Have students draw a picture of a source of pollution and another picture showing a way to stop that pollution. Students should label their pictures. Provide time for students to share their pictures with one another.

Writing

Have students think of a polluted place in their community. Challenge them to write a letter to their community leaders asking their help in cleaning up and preventing the pollution.

Art

Have students work together to make posters or a brochure showing ways that students can take part in cleaning up their school and home neighborhoods and caring for the environment. You may want to have students present the completed posters or brochure to the principal and ask to have the items displayed in school for all students.

UNIT 5 — Living Together in Neighborhoods (pages 86–102)

Unit Summary Our neighbors come from all over the United States and the world. People of different nationalities celebrate different holidays and make foods that are popular in the country from which they came. There are many ways to celebrate holidays.

Before Reading the Unit Introduce the unit by writing a few "borrowed" words on the chalkboard, such as *menu* (French), *canyon* (Spanish), *hamburger* (German), *chocolate* (Aztec American Indian), and *skunk* (American Indian). Explain that these words were borrowed from languages other than English. The people who speak these languages live in our neighborhoods, and their words are now part of English that everyone speaks. Have students read the unit opener and discuss the photograph. How do students think the photograph represents neighbors having fun together? Ask students what the neighbors are doing and what special occasion the neighbors might be celebrating. Tell them to read the questions. Ask them to look for answers as they read the unit.

Point out the Unit Project box and discuss the work students will be doing on this project.

Unit Project

Setting Up the Project Urge students to learn about holidays that are celebrated by people from other countries. If necessary, you might provide books or other resources about some of these holidays. Tell students that they will find specific suggestions for working on their projects in the Project Tip sections of the chapters. Encourage them to adapt the suggestions to their own interests.

Presenting the Project As an alternative to the project suggestion on page 102, have the team choose one holiday and create a mural that shows the steps in preparing for and celebrating the holiday.

After Reading the Unit Ask students if they were surprised by the things they learned in this unit. Why or why not? Urge them to discuss the questions asked on the unit opener. Ask additional questions, such as: How do people who come to the United States from other countries help make our neighborhoods better? Why is it good

for people to share their holidays? How does learning about the kinds of celebrations other countries have help us learn about a country's people and their way of life?

Skill Builder
Using a Time Line

After students read page 101, remind them that a time line is helpful because it shows at a glance when events take place and in what order. For example, students can tell immediately that the Pumpkin Show takes place in October. They can tell that the Great Train, Dollhouse, and Toy Show happen before the Frog Rodeo.

Answers: 1. Pumpkin Show **2.** Pennsylvania **3.** June

Bibliography
Teacher
Elbow, Gary. *How to Help Children Become Geographically Literate.* NCGE.
Low, Alice (compiler). *The Family Read-Aloud Holiday Treasury.* Little Brown, 1991.
Rice, Melanie and Chris. *All About Things People Do.* Doubleday, 1990.

Student
Bailey, Donna. *New Year in Japan.* (My World Series) Steck-Vaughn, 1990. (Grades 2–3)
Bailey, Donna. *A Mexican Festival.* (My World Series) Steck-Vaughn, 1990. (Grades 2–3)
Chin, Steven A. *Dragon Parade: A Chinese New Year Story.* (Stories of America Series) Steck-Vaughn, 1993. (Grade 2)
Dawson, Zoe. *China.* (Postcards from the World Series) Steck-Vaughn, 1996. (Grades 2–3)
Humphrey, Paul. *People Everywhere.* (Read All About It Series) Steck-Vaughn, 1995. (Grade 2)
Nielsen, Shelly. *Independence Day.* (Holiday Celebrations Series) Abdo and Daughters, 1991. (Grades 1–3)

Teacher's Resource Binder

Blackline Masters for Unit 5: Unit 5 Project Organizer, Unit 5 Review, Unit 5 Test; Activities for Chapters 11, 12; Outline Map of the World

Chapter Summary The people in our neighborhoods come from many places. They speak different languages and have different traditions. They bring their different cultures with them to America and share them with the people here.

Chapter Objectives Students will learn to

- identify ways in which people are alike and different.
- read a world map and identify neighboring countries.
- recognize ways in which people from other countries celebrate their holidays.

Vocabulary

citizen, p. 92

Vocabulary Activities Write the vocabulary word *citizen* on the chalkboard and say it aloud. Ask volunteers to share their understanding of the word. Discuss what a good citizen does (obeys laws of the country, votes in elections, works to make the neighborhood and country better). Encourage students to draw pictures that illustrate ways they can be good citizens.

Before Reading the Chapter Remind students of the Pilgrims they learned about in Chapter 4. Tell students that since that time, millions of people have moved to the United States. If students know about their ethnic backgrounds, invite them to share this information. Compile a list of the countries from which you, your students, or their ancestors have come. As students become comfortable using the world map, have them find the countries listed on the map.

Teaching Suggestions and Answers
Page 87
Ask students to look at the picture. Prompt students to think of ways that people are alike by asking these questions: What do all these people need in order to live? (food, clothing, shelter) Who do these people live with? (their families) What do you think they do with their families? (play, work, share family celebrations)

Discuss with students that people from all countries are alike in many ways. **Answers may include that these people all have the same needs: they look different from each other, may speak different languages, and may live in different kinds of homes.**

Page 88
Assist students in becoming familiar with the world map on pages 88 and 89. Point out the compass rose and review with them how it shows the cardinal directions. Help them locate the United States, pointing out that both Alaska and Hawaii are part of the United States. Ask students: On what continent is the United States found? (North America) Is Mexico north or south of the United States? (south) On what continent is China found? (Asia) You may want to point out that not all countries of the world are shown on this map. **Students should draw a green circle around the United States, including Alaska and Hawaii. They should draw a line under the name of Mexico. They should put a *C* on the continent of South America.**

Page 89
Students should draw a purple circle around Canada. They should draw a blue circle around China. They should identify the ocean east of China as the Pacific Ocean. Ask students: What countries are shown in Africa? (Chad, Ghana, Nigeria) What countries are shown in Europe? (France, Italy) What continent is the farthest south? (Antarctica)

Page 90
Discuss with students how many people follow traditions, or customs, from other countries even though they have been in the United States for many years. Many people who are born in the United States continue traditions brought to this country by their ancestors. Invite students to speculate about why people follow these traditions. Encourage volunteers to tell about traditions their families practice. Extend the discussion by inviting students to tell about things they know about that have come from other countries. Prompt them by asking them about foods

(Italian food, Chinese food, Mexican food, and so on) and festivals. **Students should write a question they would like answered about a fiesta. Questions will vary, but may include questions about the kinds of food, games, and dances at a fiesta.**

Page 91

Have students look at each of the pictures and identify things that they do not see in their own neighborhood. Have them tell what things are the same. Ask students: Why are the signs in both English and Chinese? (Some people from China might not be able to read English yet.) **Answers will vary. Possible responses include that both neighborhoods have places to buy food, to work, and to live.**

Project Tip

Help students carry out the suggestion on page 91. If any adults at the school celebrate traditional holidays from other countries, you might invite them to the classroom to answer questions about how they celebrate these holidays.

Page 92

Did You Know? Explain to students that the usual waiting period before people apply for United States citizenship is five years. To help students appreciate what new citizens should know, give them a sample citizenship test, asking, How do we elect the President? Who is the President? When do we celebrate our country's birthday? You might discuss with students what it means to be a good citizen. Explain that good citizenship includes obeying the laws of the community and country, voting in elections, and doing things to make the community and country better places to live. **Students should write one thing they think a new citizen of the United States should know. Answers will vary.**

Page 93

Chapter Checkup You may want to work through the Chapter Checkup with students.

Answers: 1. world **2.** country **3.** neighbors **4.** citizen
Encourage students to volunteer their ideas. Answers will vary, but students should demonstrate an understanding that these people

bring different ways of doing things, and these differences help make the United States more interesting.

After Reading the Chapter

Point out to students that many of the foods we eat originally came from other countries. Help them make a list of all the foods they can learn about that came from another country. Challenge them to name foods from as many different countries as they can. Have them find each of the countries on a world map.

Writing

Have students imagine they are writing to a pen pal in another country. Students may choose to write to an imaginary pen pal in one of the countries they learned about in this chapter (Mexico, Canada, or China), or they may choose another country. Ask each student to write a letter explaining how people in the United States try to be good neighbors.

Geography

Have students plan a trip around the world. They may work as individual travelers or plan a "tour" for their group. Students should determine which languages people speak in the countries to which they travel.

Chapter Summary Neighbors celebrate many United States holidays together by having picnics, and by attending parades and other events. Two important national holidays are the Fourth of July and Columbus Day.

Chapter Objectives Students will learn to

- recognize different ways holidays are celebrated.

- identify holidays celebrated in the United States and identify the dates on which they occur.

- read a time line.

Vocabulary

celebrate, p. 94   time line, p. 96

holiday, p. 95

Vocabulary Activities Tell students that it is often helpful to remember the order in which things happen. Ask students to name some ways they remember things (write them down, draw pictures, make up a rhyme). Tell students that another way to remember when things happen is by making a time line. A time line is like a chart. Make a time line of a typical school week. Students should fill in what happens on each day. When it is complete, review the concept with students. Ask how a day is started; what happens after gym; what is done last each week. Remind students who are having difficulty with vocabulary terms to check the glossary.

Before Reading the Chapter Have students discuss any parades or fireworks displays they have seen. Ask what holiday or special time was being celebrated. Before students read pages 96–97, review the order of the months in a year. Have students look at the time line on pages 96–97. Tell them that this time line is a little bit like a calendar. It has the months written in order along the bottom. On top are the names of holidays with lines down to the months in which these holidays take place. Tell students that they will learn how to read this time line.

Teaching Suggestions and Answers

Page 94

Point out the vocabulary word *celebrate,* and discuss its meaning with students. Tell them we celebrate to honor or think about special people or events. We celebrate in many ways. Sometimes we celebrate in noisy, happy, fun ways, as on the Fourth of July. Sometimes we celebrate in quieter, more serious ways, as on some religious holidays. Invite students to name some holidays they know and tell what or who is celebrated and how people celebrate the day. Invite students to tell about parades they have seen. Ask what the parade was celebrating. Who was in the parade? What did you like best? **Students should draw a picture of a parade, showing what they liked best about it.**

Project Tip

Discuss the Project Tip with students. You may want to model the activity by telling about your own family traditions in celebrating a certain holiday. Ask students to talk about the same or another holiday. Encourage them to tell what they like about the way other classmates celebrate a holiday.

Page 95

Ask students to tell how people celebrate the Fourth of July. (People celebrate by displaying the United States flag and having parades, barbecues, picnics, fireworks, and festivals.) Tell students that the Fourth of July is officially called Independence Day. It is the birthday of the United States because on July 4, 1776, the United States declared itself a free and independent country. You might want to tell students briefly about the circumstances leading up to and immediately following that date. **Students should write an explanation for the importance of celebrating the Fourth of July. Possible response: Celebrating the Fourth of July helps people remember why freedom is important.**

Page 96

Emphasize to students that a time line can show any period of time—an hour, a month, a year, or centuries. Ask students to determine what time period is shown on this time line. (a year) Which month is the first month of the year? (January) What kind of events are shown on this time line? (holidays) **Students should respond that February comes right after January. They should identify January as the month with two holidays.**

Page 97

Students should respond that Thanksgiving is in November. They should circle Columbus Day on the time line. They should add their birthday to the time line. They should add a holiday that their family celebrates to the time line.

Page 98

Special People The book referred to in the text is *Family Pictures/Cuadros de familia*, Children's Book Press, 1990. You may wish to obtain a copy of the book to read and to show to students. *Family Pictures* is in English and Spanish and includes lively illustrations drawn by the author. Tell students that Lomas Garza grew up in a small town in Texas near the Mexican border. Assist students in finding Texas and Mexico on the United States map on pages 104–105. Lomas Garza's family followed many Mexican traditions when celebrating holidays. As a young girl, Lomas Garza dreamed of becoming an artist, and practiced drawing every day. The pictures of her family, neighbors, and family life in *Family Pictures* were drawn from her memories of growing up. Invite students to tell what they want to do when they grow up. You might also encourage students to draw pictures of family or neighborhood celebrations they have experienced. **Students should tell the name of a holiday they would like to write about.**

Page 99

You may wish to tell students that the Chinese New Year begins between January 21 and February 19. On the last night, some people dress up as dragons and hold a parade. Direct attention to the photographs. The picture on the left shows children dancing at a festival in Sweden. The picture on the right is of a festival parade in Colombia. You may wish to have students locate these countries on a world map or globe. Also help them find Belgium and China. **Students should respond that the people are dancing and having a parade.**

Page 100

Chapter Checkup Make sure all students understand what the correct answers are to the numbered questions.

Answers: 1. T **2.** F **3.** T **4.** T
Invite students to volunteer answers to the question. Answers will vary, but students should correctly identify the person or event celebrated on the holiday they like best, and should give a reason why it is important to remember this person or event.

After Reading the Chapter

Challenge students to draw a time line of their lives. The time line should begin with the year in which they were born and end at the present time. Have students include important events in their lives, such as when they started school, when a sibling was born, when they moved, or when they got a pet.

Writing

Have students write a short story about their favorite holiday. Suggest that they base their stories on actual family events.

Music

Encourage students to learn a folk song that comes from another country. Have them sing or recite the song for their classmates.

Cultural Geography

Have students "interview" a classmate or an adult who retains some traditions or culture from another country. Have students ask about special holidays celebrated in that country. Invite students to share what they learned with the rest of the class.

Date _____

Dear Family:

During this school year, your child will be studying neighbors and neighborhoods by using the book *People and Places Nearby*. This book is divided into five units. The first unit, which we are now completing, introduced the neighborhood as a place where people live, work, and play. Your child learned that neighborhoods are found in different geographic places and that neighborhoods are continually changing.

You can help reinforce what your child has learned by looking at the book with your child. Ask your child to tell you about the pictures and maps. You might ask him or her to read a few pages to you.

Below are listed several additional activities that you might want to do with your child to support our study of this unit.

Thank you for your interest and support.

Sincerely,

_____

A Walk Around the Neighborhood

Take a walk around your neighborhood with your child. Point out and list the many different activities you see neighbors doing.

Our Changing Neighborhood

Choose something in your neighborhood that is undergoing a change. It could be a building demolition or renovation, new construction, clean-up of an empty lot, or the planting of trees and flowers. Have your child draw or take photographs of the changes at various stages.

Getting to School

Help your child make a simple picture map of his or her route to school. Write the street names and draw pictures of buildings on the map. Walk your child through the map, using direction terms such as north, south, east, and west. You might even go for a walk to school and use the map as a guide.

Fecha _____

Estimada familia:

Durante este año escolar, su hijo o hija usará el libro *People and Places Nearby* para estudiar los vecinos y sus vecindarios. El libro está dividido en cinco unidades. Ya casi hemos terminado con la primera unidad, la cual describe el vecindario como un lugar donde la gente vive, trabaja y se divierte. Su hijo o hija ya ha aprendido que los vecindarios se encuentran en distintas regiones geográficas y que los vecindarios cambian continuamente.

Usted puede ayudar a su hijo o hija a reforzar en casa lo que estamos estudiando en la escuela. Para hacerlo, anímelo a conversar acerca de los dibujos y los mapas de la unidad que estamos estudiando. También puede pedirle que le lea unas cuantas páginas del libro.

A continuación encontrará varias actividades adicionales para hacer con su hijo o hija con las que pueden ampliar el estudio de esta unidad.

Muchas gracias por su interés y su apoyo.

Atentamente,

_____

Un paseo por el vecindario

Tome un paseo por su vecindario con su hijo o hija. Señálele la gran variedad de actividades que pueden hacer con los vecinos. Preparen una lista de todas estas actividades.

Nuestro vecindario cambiante

Escojan un lugar de su vecindario que esté cambiando. Podría ser la demolición o renovación de un edificio, una construcción nueva, la limpieza de un lote vacío o un proyecto de plantar árboles y flores. Pídale a su hijo o hija que dibuje o que tome fotografías de los cambios en sus diferentes etapas.

La ruta escolar

Ayude a su hijo o hija a dibujar un mapa simple de su ruta para ir a la escuela. Escriban los nombres de las calles y hagan dibujos de los edificios en el mapa. Repasen juntos la ruta en el mapa, usando términos de dirección, como norte sur, este y oeste. Si lo desean, pueden dar un paseo hasta la escuela y usar el mapa como guía.

Date _____

Dear Family:

Your child is now completing Unit 2 of *People and Places Nearby*. In this unit, we have learned that American Indians were the first people to live in America. Students also learned something about the ways American Indians lived. Your child also studied Columbus and the early English settlers of America.

To reinforce what your child has learned, invite him or her to tell you how American Indians lived in America long ago. You might ask your child to show you the pictures of American Indians and to tell you what the pictures show. You might also ask your child to tell you about the Pilgrims and how they lived when they first arrived.

Below are some additional activities you might do with your child.

Thank you for your support.

Sincerely,

_____

Tell Me a Story

Help your child learn more about what your neighborhood was like long ago by talking to older members of the community.

My Family Long Ago

Tell your child about your family history. Share what you know about when and how your family came to America and where the family lived before. Ask older family members to tell what they know about the family.

Carta a las Familias

Fecha _____

Estimada familia:

    Su hijo o hija continúa aprendiendo sobre las familias en general, mientras estudiamos la Unidad 2 de *People and Places Nearby*. En esta unidad aprendemos que los indios americanos fueron los primeros habitantes en lo que hoy es los Estados Unidos. Los estudiantes también han aprendido algo sobre la vida de los indios americanos. También han estudiado acerca de Cristobal Colón y los primeros ingleses que llegaron a Norte América.

    Usted puede ayudar a su hijo o hija a reforzar en casa lo que hemos estudiado en la escuela. Para hacerlo, invítelo a contarle cómo vivían en Norte América los indios americanos hace mucho tiempo. Le puede pedir que le muestre las ilustraciones del libro y que las explique. También puede pedirle que le cuente sobre los Peregrinos y cómo vivían cuando llegaron a Norte América.

    A continuación aparecen varias actividades adicionales que puede hacer con su hijo o hija.

    Muchas gracias por su apoyo.

Atentamente,

_____

Cuéntame un cuento

    Ayude a que su hijo o hija aprenda más sobre cómo era hace mucho tiempo el vecindario en que viven. Para hacerlo, conversen con personas ya mayores que hayan vivido por bastante tiempo en la comunidad.

Mi familia de tiempos pasados

    Cuéntele a su hijo o hija sobre la historia de su familia. Comparta con él o ella lo que usted sabe sobre cuándo y cómo llegó su familia a los Estados Unidos y de dónde proviene la familia. Pídales a los miembros mayores de su familia que cuenten lo que saben sobre la historia de la familia.

Date _____

Dear Family:

Your child's class is now completing study of Unit 3 of *People and Places Nearby*. In this unit, your child learned about the different kinds of jobs people do and about the goods and services workers provide.

You can help your child understand and remember this material by asking him or her to read some of the pages to you and to explain the graphs and pictures. Encourage your child to tell you about the different jobs that people have.

You may also want to do one of the following activities with your child.

Thank you for your interest and support.

Sincerely,

_____

What to Buy?

Plan your weekly grocery list with your child. Discuss which items you need and which you want. Talk about how your decisions about what to buy are based on how much money you have to spend.

Be a Volunteer!

Volunteer with your child to do some service for your community, such as participating in a clean-up day or collecting food for a food bank or soup kitchen.

Fecha _____

Estimada familia:

La clase de su hijo o hija está ahora completando sus estudios de la Unidad 3 del libro *People and Places Nearby*. En esta unidad, han aprendido sobre las distintas clases de trabajo que hace la gente y sobre los bienes y servicios que proporcionan los trabajadores.

Para ayudar a su hijo o hija a comprender y recordar este material, puede pedirle que le lea en voz alta algunas de las páginas que haya leído y que le explique las gráficas y los dibujos en esas páginas. Anímelo a que le explique la diferencia entre los distintos tipos de trabajos que tiene la gente.

También puede hacer una de las siguientes actividades con su hijo o hija.

Muchas gracias por su interés y su apoyo.

Atentamente,

_____

¿Qué comprar?

Junto con su hijo o hija prepare la lista semanal de mercado. Decidan cuáles artículos son verdaderamente necesarios y cuáles no. Conversen sobre cómo las decisiones sobre lo que se va a comprar dependen de cuánto dinero tienen para gastar.

¡De voluntarios!

Ofrézcanse con su hijo o hija de voluntarios para algún servicio de la comunidad. Por ejemplo, pueden participar en un día de limpieza o recolectar alimentos para un banco de alimentos que da de comer a la gente pobre.

Date _____

Dear Family:

Your child is now completing Unit 4 of *People and Places Nearby*. This unit discussed rules and laws and how we need them to keep things safe, clean, and fair. Students learned about the ways in which people make and change laws and learned about some of our leaders, such as the mayor, governor, and President.

You can help your child master this material by discussing the chapters with him or her. Invite your child to tell what he or she has learned and to name the President and other government leaders.

You may also want to do one or more of the following activities with your child. They will help build your child's understanding of the themes of this unit.

Thank you for your help and interest.

Sincerely,

_____

Rules for Our Family

Make a poster with your child to help him or her remember family rules. These might include clean-up rules, bedtime rules, safety rules, and so on.

Signs All Around Us

Many signs in the community remind us of the rules and laws that help us live together. Point out these reminders to your child, and discuss what the rule or law is and why it is important.

Carta a las Familias

Fecha _____

Estimada familia:

Ahora su hijo o hija está completando la Unidad 4 de *People and Places Nearby*. En esta unidad estamos hablando de las reglas y de las leyes, y del por qué las necesitamos para mantener un nivel adecuado de protección, limpieza e igualdad. Los estudiantes han aprendido sobre las maneras en que la gente hace y cambia las leyes y también han estudiado sobre algunos de nuestros líderes, tales como el alcalde, el gobernador y el presidente.

Usted puede ayudar a su hijo o hija a conocer a fondo este material. Para hacerlo, invítelo a decirle lo que ha aprendido y pídale que nombre al presidente y a otros líderes del gobierno.

También puede hacer con su hijo o hija una o más de las actividades que aparecen a continuación. Estas actividades le ayudarán a establecer la comprensión que su hijo o hija necesita de los temas de esta unidad.

Muchas gracias por su interés y su apoyo.

Atentamente,

_____

Las reglas de nuestra familia

Prepare un cartel con su hijo o hija que le ayude a él o ella a recordar las reglas de la familia. Las reglas podrían incluir, por ejemplo: las reglas de limpieza, las reglas sobre la hora de acostarse y las reglas de seguridad.

Los letreros a nuestro alrededor

Muchos de los letreros de la comunidad nos hacen recordar las reglas y las leyes que nos ayudan a vivir juntos. Señale a su hijo o hija algunos letreros y conversen sobre la regla o la ley que contiene cada uno y su importancia.

Date _____

Dear Family:

Your child is now studying the final unit of *People and Places Nearby*. Students learned how neighbors come from all over the United States and all over the world. Your child learned how people from these different places bring their own holiday traditions and special foods with them. We will study ways in which neighbors celebrate and share their holidays.

You can reinforce your child's learning experience by talking about the pictures, maps, and charts in Unit 5 of the book. Ask your child to explain what the time line shows.

You might also consider helping your child complete one of the following activities. These activities will give your child additional understanding of the topics we are studying in this unit.

Thank you for your interest and support.

Sincerely,

_____

Let's Celebrate!

Have your child assist in the planning of a family holiday. This may involve planning and preparing the food or making decorations and invitations.

Food from Around the World

Experiment with making various ethnic dishes from other countries, or take your child out to eat at ethnic restaurants in your neighborhood. Discuss where the food originated and how it is similar to and different from the food your family usually eats.

Carta a las Familias

Fecha _____

Estimada familia:

Ahora su hijo o hija está completando sus estudios de la última unidad de *People and Places Nearby*. Los estudiantes han aprendido que nuestros vecinos vienen de todas partes de los Estados Unidos y de todas partes del mundo. Su hijo o hija ha aprendido como las personas de distintos lugares traen consigo sus propias tradiciones de fiestas y comidas especiales. Ahora vamos a estudiar las maneras en que los distintos vecinos celebran y comparten sus fiestas tradicionales.

Puede ayudar a reforzar la experiencia de aprendizaje de su hijo o hija conversando sobre las ilustraciones, los mapas y las gráficas de la Unidad 5 del libro. Pídale a su hijo o hija que le explique lo que muestra la línea del tiempo.

También puede considerar ayudar a su hijo o hija a completar una de las siguientes actividades. Estas actividades le darán a su hijo o hija comprensión adicional de los temas que hemos estudiado en esta unidad.

Gracias por su interés y su apoyo.

Atentamente,

_____

¡A celebrar!

Pídale a su hijo o hija que le ayude a planear una fiesta familiar. En su planificación puede incluir la preparación de la comida, de las decoraciones y de las invitaciones.

Comidas de todas partes del mundo

Preparen platos de distintos países o lleve a su hijo o hija a comer en restaurantes en su vecindario que sirvan comida de diferentes países. Conversen sobre dónde se originó cada comida y en qué se parece o se diferencia de las comidas que come su familia normalmente.

Name _____

STECK-VAUGHN
C O M P A N Y
ELEMENTARY • SECONDARY • ADULT • LIBRARY

ISBN 0-8172-6557-0

9 780817 265571

90000

Homes and Families